D1756635

PRODUCT DESIGN AND CORPORATE STRATEGY

PRODUCT DESIGN AND CORPORATE STRATEGY

Managing the Connection for Competitive Advantage

Robert Blaich with Janet Blaich

McGraw-Hill, Inc.

New York San Francisco Washington, D.C. Auckland Bogotá
Caracas Lisbon London Madrid Mexico City
Milan Montreal New Delhi San Juan
Singapore Sydney Tokyo Toronto

Library of Congress Cataloging-in-Publication Data

Blaich, Robert.
    Product design and corporate strategy : managing the connection
for competitive advantage / Robert Blaich with Janet Blaich.
        p.   cm.
    Includes index.
    ISBN 0-07-005671-4
    1. New products—United States—Management.   2. Product
management—United States.   3. Design, Industrial—United States.
I. Blaich, Janet.   II. Title.
HF5415.153.B57   1993
658.5′75—dc20   92-30462
                                                              CIP

1 2 3 4 5 6 7 8 9 0   DOH/DOH   9 8 7 6 5 4 3 2

ISBN   0-07-005671-4

*The sponsoring editor for this book was Karen Hansen, the editing
supervisor was Jane Palmieri, the designer was Sue Maksuta, and the
production supervisor was Donald Schmidt. It was set in Times by
McGraw-Hill's Professional Book Group composition unit.*

Printed and bound by R. R. Donnelley & Sons Company.

This book is printed on recycled, acid-free paper containing a minimum of 50% recycled de-
inked fiber.

The following Herman Miller products referred to in this book are
registered trademark names:
  Action Factory
  Action Office
  Action Office 2
  Burdick System
  Coherent Structures (Co/Struc)
  Eames Contract Storage
  Eames Educational Seating
  Eames Tandem Seating
  Equa and Ergon Chairs
  Nelson CSS

Contents

Foreword   ix
Preface   xi

Introduction   **1**

Part 1. Bringing Design into the Management Mainstream

1. What Is Design Management?   **7**

Why Is Managing Design Different from Managing Anything Else?   7
Distinguishing Between Design Activities   8
   Product Design   8
   Communications Design   9
   Environment Design   9
Structuring Design Activities for Synergistic Impact   10
Getting It Straight about Designers and Engineers   10
Design Management as a New Discipline   12
The Tasks of Design Management   13
Repeat: Design Management Is Specific to Design Activity   16
References   17

2. Design: The New Competitive Trump Card   **18**

Design Management Emerges as a New Discipline   18
   The Rise of Globalism   19
   The Empowered Consumer   20
   Product Differentiation: Battle Cry of the 1990s   20
Waking Up to the Importance of Design   21
Learning More from Japan Than How to Manufacture   23

Soft Values as the Focus of Lifestyle Research   24
Government Commitment to Design in Other Countries   27
Concentrating the Minds of Business Executives on Design   29
References   31

3. Ten Design Management Issues and How They Connect to Corporate Strategy   32

1. The Status of Design in Corporations   33
2. Design as a Strategic Factor for Achieving Corporate Goals   34
3. Expanding the Scope of Design Work   35
4. Full Integration of Design in the Product Creation Process   36
5. Design-Led Innovation as Stimulus to Product Creation   36
6. Management of Corporate Design Resources   37
7. Managing a Global Design Organization   38
8. Design as a Force for Quality   39
9. Who Should Be a Design Manager?   39
10. Developing Design Management Training Resources   42
References   43

Part 2. Herman Miller and Design Management

4. Herman Miller and the "Providential" Partnership with Design   47

From "Princess" Bureaus to Leading-Edge Modernism   48
Pioneering a Corporate Identity Program   49
Linking Design and Marketing   50
Design Leads the Company to New Businesses   51
Design and the Multimillion-Dollar Office Business   53
At Issue: Consultants or In-House Design Staff   55
Design Managed by Marketers   58
References   59

5. Herman Miller Case Studies and Design Management Issues   60

Case Study: Eames Contract Storage (ECS)   60
     ECS and Design Management Issues   63
Case Study: Eames Educational Seating (EES)   65
     EES and Design Management Issues   67
Case Study: Eames Tandem Seating   69
     Tandem Seating and Design Management Issues   71

Case Study: Action Office 2 (AO2)   73
             AO2 and Design Management Issues   80
Case Study: Corporate Identity at Herman Miller   81
             Corporate Design and Communications and Design
               Management Issues   85
References   87

Part 3. Philips and Design Management

6. Plugging in Design as a Global Strategy   91

Design as a Cottage Industry Around the World   92
Redesigning the Design Organization   94
Design: From a Cottage Industry to a Global Organization   96
Letting the Designers Manage   98
  Defining Who Designers Are and What They Do   99
  Managing the Design Process   102
Improving Professional Standards   103
  Giving Designers the Tools They Need   106
  Team Approach to Stimulating New Thinking   107
Creating a Corporate Identity   110
Does the Design Process Have to Be Messy?   110
Separating the Egg Without Piercing the Yolk   113
References   115

7. Philips Case Studies and Design Management Issues   118

Case Study: Harmonization Program   118
             The Harmonization Program and Design Management Issues   123
Case Study: Design for Market   124
             Design for Market and Design Management Issues   127
Case Study: Youth Task Force: Product Planning and Design for Youth   128
             Youth Program and Design Management Issues   133
Case Study: Consumer Luminaires   134
             Consumer Luminaires and Design Management Issues   137
Case Study: Integris C   138
             Integris C and Design Management Issues   141
Case Study: Videophone   143
             Videophone and Design Management Issues   146
Case Study: ROTA '90 Shaver Series   148
             ROTA '90 and Design Management Issues   150
Case Study: The Philips Collection   152
             The Philips Collection and Design Management Issues   155

Case Study: The Evoluon   156
    The Evoluon and Design Management Issues   161

Part 4. A Basis for Building a Design Management Methodology

8. Design Management and Some Common Ground for All Companies   165

Structure Matters   166
Getting the Order of Things Right   167
Sending Designers Out from the Center   168
How to Choose: In-House Design Staff or Consultants?   170
  It's Not Necessarily a Case of Either/Or   172
Infusing a Little Outside Objectivity   175
Summing Up: Design Management Common Ground for All Companies 176

9. The Fertile Ground Factor   178

Creating a Corporate Culture for Design to Flourish   178
What Makes the Ground Fertile?   179
Communicate! Communicate! Communicate!   181
Reaching the High Ground: Dedication to a Corporate Identity Program 182
Who Should Till the Fertile Ground?   183
References   186

Index   187

Foreword

Design—for those organizations that are still viable in the midst of intense global competition and economic turbulence—can be a powerful resource for survival. Most competition is no longer based on time-to-market, quality, or price; as Norio Ohga, president of Sony, recently said, "Design may soon be the only element that differentiates one product from another." Professor Robert Hayes of the Harvard Business School says, "Design represents not simply a new frontier for management, but the next frontier for industrial competition."

Furthermore, as products have proliferated, consumers worldwide find they have unprecedented choice in the marketplace. Price and quality are often virtually equal, giving design the job of differentiating products and influencing the purchase decision. Effective design contributions go far beyond the simple selection of color or trim to core issues like performance, durability, intelligibility, usability, and an appearance that not only pleases but informs. Design also contributes to making responsible products that are safe to use and environmentally appropriate.

From the business side, design awareness is growing. *Business Week* in the last few years has increased its coverage of design fivefold. *Fortune, The Wall Street Journal*, and other business publications have followed its lead. Understanding just what a design resource is, however—how to structure it and how to utilize it—has lagged behind this new interest.

Along with this growth in design awareness, initiatives to bring more design into industry have emerged in Europe and the Far East. For example, in the early eighties Great Britain sponsored innovative and well-funded programs in design consulting for industry in an effort to augment the British economy. Following these programs, Professor Robin Roy at the Open University led a research effort to substantiate the results of investing in design. For a range of projects his research showed an average payback period of less than 16 months. This was a rather impressive feat, since the typical payback period for investment in development resources is around 36 months.

At the dawn of the nineties we saw Japan declare 1989 a "Year of Design."

Through the Ministry of International Trade and Industry, the Japanese initiated an impressive range of design programs throughout virtually every facet of Japanese industry and society. Each of the 47 prefectures was required to open a design center, thus creating—almost overnight—an infrastructure for promoting and supporting design in industry. No other nation has made this kind or level of commitment. Clearly, this approach reflects Japan's understanding of the power of design and its desire to embed design within the very fabric of its economy. Following this example, Taiwan, Singapore, Korea, Malaysia, Spain, and other countries are investing millions to bring effective design into their industries.

Short of massive public investments, how can design become a part of corporate strategy? What happens behind the scenes where award-winning products are consistently developed? How can design help build a sustainable competitive advantage?

This book gives the reader a look behind the scenes, through the eyes of a seasoned design manager, at two design-driven, world-class companies. It provides a rare view of how industry leaders use design as a strategy weapon, and suggests how almost any company can benefit from their experience.

Earl N. Powell
Director
Design Management Institute

Preface

Describing design and its management in terms such as *strategic, competitive weapon*, and *value-added advantage* might understandably cause reactions of bemusement, if not skepticism. After all, in the minds of most people, including business managers, design has something to do with how things look. Yes, it's important that the products a company sells look good and that the company's ads look sophisticated, catchy, or sober, depending on the ad strategy of the year. But design is not in the same hardball league as strategic issues such as price, quality, time-to-market, or technology innovation. Or is it?

There must surely be a link between design and the current public discussion about product competitiveness. That link, certainly not a mystery to the companies who are causing all the anxiety with their relentless march on market share, is the underlying subject of this book. But even if the arguments for paying serious attention to design and its link to competitiveness are persuasive, what then? What does a company do about improving the design of its products and communications? The simple answer is companies have to learn how to manage design to achieve competitive results.

The concept of a discipline for managing design has been around for quite some time, but real and considerable interest in the process of design within corporations and the development of methodologies for integrating it into the strategic and operational activities of companies is quickening. This new interest in design management is widespread. It is being discussed in all the industrialized countries of the world. Governments, universities, and industry are taking some kind of action to accumulate research on how corporations are dealing with the design process and on how to teach a design management methodology.

I have participated and continue to be involved in many of these discussions and formulations for action in developing design management as a discipline for business. These deliberations are conducted in a variety of venues and are sponsored by governments, academic institutions, and design and business organizations from Finland to Brazil, from Taiwan to South Africa. As a speaker at these conferences, symposia, or roundtable discussions, I nearly always wish more time were available to properly get beneath my overview presentation to the details that would amplify and explain the general observations made necessary by time constraints. I would like to tell more of the story in the hope that some of the people in the audience can make a connection with it to help them in their own situation.

With the encouragement of many of my professional peers, I decided to try to tell about design management as I have experienced it in the last 30 years. The heart of this book is that story—not a history of my experiences, nor a history of the companies with which I was involved, except as these relate to the design function in the company. It is, rather, a compendium of case studies about design projects and the establishment of design programs, each of which tells something that I think is worthwhile about the process of managing design in the corporate environment.

The telling of these stories in a case study format is not intended to imply that this is the only way design management should be carried out. The case studies describe *one* way to manage design, not *the* way to do it. Not all projects were successful in their resolution, but something worthwhile was learned that later benefited the design management process. Readers, I believe, will have glimmers of recognition, seeing similarities in the situations described with problems they've faced. But in true creative style, readers will adapt the process I describe to fit their own management styles, their own problems, their own companies.

Something should also be said about design management relative to the size of a company. I have often felt in recent years when giving presentations that many people in the audience might feel intimidated about the discussion of Philips' design operations by virtue of the size of the design group, the size of Philips itself, and the scope of its products. I think the case studies, presented in more depth in the book than is possible in a half-hour general topic presentation at a conference, will strike cords of familiarity: "That reminds me of something I went through!" I have swapped stories often enough with fellow designers to know that large or small, whatever the business is, situations have problems and characteristics in common.

I also have had design management experience in a small company. When I joined Herman Miller it was a very small company indeed. Its annual turnover in 1953 was less than $3 million. Even by the end of 1979, when it had grown to an annual sales volume of $230 million, I still knew almost everyone in the company by name, including the people in the factory. Herman Miller and Philips could not have been more different even though they are both Dutch in their origins. Their size, what they produced, and, more strikingly, the company culture were dramatically different during the times of my association with them. Yet I could often draw parallels in the anatomy of specific situations. And so, although design management must be flexible and dynamic in its methodology, some common bases exist to build a discipline for developing an effective interface with other functional and operational disciplines within corporations.

The first and last parts of this book enfold the Herman Miller and Philips sections. The first part places the descriptions of Herman Miller and Philips in the context of what design management is, how design has been perceived by business and industry, and how the tumultuous economic, social, and political changes we are experiencing have contributed to the growing interest in design as a strategic factor in competitive battles. The last chapter in Part 1 lays out ten critical design management issues for all companies.

The final part, the other bracket to the case studies, discusses the common ground that exists in companies, regardless of size or scope of product range, for conducting a managed design process. Timely issues related to structuring a design organization, whether to build a design program around an in-house staff or consultants, and maintaining responsiveness to company change for dealing with aspects of structural change such as decentralization are all elements of "common ground" matters.

Finally, the subject of design and the corporate culture is addressed as the "fertile ground factor." Design leadership is the key to maintaining an effective, managed design process. Who should provide design leadership in a company? This is a subject of strenuous debate. The last chapter points out that reaching a consensus on this issue among educators, designers, and business managers will be paramount to the success of the practice of design management.

The emphasis throughout this book is on product design, but as my role in design management at Herman Miller demonstrates, I am a strong proponent of the management of design as a holistic activity that combines product, communications, and environment design. I faced a number of serious problems when I joined Philips, and I had to set priorities for action. By the time I stepped down as director of design at the end of 1991, the support for design and the comprehension of its value to Philips was such that, with good design management, the integration of all aspects of design has the possibility to be achieved in the next few years.

Thus, a major theme of this book is that the design activity is broader in scope than merely product design. All aspects of design must be interactive, supportive, and harmonious in their expressions to present a coherent identity to a company's various constituents. This orchestration is what design management is all about.

Robert Blaich

INTRODUCTION

The term *design management* has a sound about it that is appealing to nondesigners—especially business managers. The suggestion that something as abstract as design can be managed is a welcome idea to business people, many of whom cannot stand the ambiguity that characterizes the design activity in their companies. But what is design management? Does a company really need to acquire yet another management skill specialty?

The reasons for a more thorough examination of how the design activity is conducted in companies are beginning to mount, and the arguments for the importance of design to businesses are coming from many sources and directions. Design management—what it is and its relevance to current business strategies and operations—has become part of the discourse on product quality improvement and achieving competitive advantage.

In their broadest sense, the diverse aspects of design are pervasive in the human-made environment. All the artifacts of living—working, playing, learning, traveling, maintaining health—have been designed by someone, made and sold by some company. Everyone knows this. But very few business managers in the past gave much consideration to the activity of design in the conduct of their business. The proportion of attention given to design in relation to technology research, finance, manufacturing, marketing, and distribution has been minuscule. The effects of design have always been taught, analyzed, and strategically planned for in other terms. Business managers, academicians, and economic analysts express those as profit, trade balances, quality, production efficiencies, consumer demand, added value, customer satisfaction, and so on.

Even though the designer shapes the form of the product; influences the materials used; defines the user interaction with the product; and affects the utility, cost, and methods of production, for many years he or she clearly has had relatively little influence on the strategic thinking of companies. Nor have designers been key players in the operational management of the product creation process. By the time the designer becomes involved, all the important decisions have already been made. The designer, who is essentially a problem solver and therefore should be proactive, has in practice been mostly rendered reactive. The operational policies and procedures of most companies, which place designers near the end of the product development sequence of activities, effectively reduce designers' potential for making a significant contribution to corporate goals and objectives.

I have heard years of anecdotal evidence at design conferences to support these observations about how design functions in most corporations. It is little wonder that many designers in the past suffered from acute inferiority complexes.

But this dismal state of affairs for both designers and businesses is changing.

Designers themselves, both individually and collectively, have gotten more adept at presenting the case for the benefits of better use of design in business operations. ICSID (the International Council of Societies of Industrial Design) at last count registered some 250 organizations both public and private devoted to the promotion of design or the encouragement of its professionalization. Many of these design promotion organizations are seriously supported by governments.

Business publications and mass media in the past several years have become design advocates. This welcome development can be credited to an improved articulation by designers about the role of design, but perhaps even more significantly, the interest of journalists has been sparked by the connection they are making between economic developments and design.

In the mid-1980s, Christopher Lorenz, editor of the management page of the *Financial Times* (London), began to write influential articles about the role of design in business, usually in articles describing product design management in specific companies.

The Wall Street Journal also began to run feature articles in the 1980s about design and business, and *Time Magazine* added a design department to its editorial staff to produce regular features on the subject. *Time* now includes a section on design in its annual best-of-year issue. More recently *Business Week* has weighed in with a regular design editorial department, launching the new department with the now often-quoted prediction that design would be to the 1990s what finance was to the 1980s and marketing was to the 1970s. Both *Business Week* and the *Financial Times* extended their editorial interest in design: The *Financial Times* sponsored a conference for business managers on design issues of the 1990s, and the Industrial Designers Society of America (IDSA) and *Business Week* now cosponsor an annual design award program to business. By the end of the 1980s designers had moved beyond talking only to themselves in their own publications to the more influential domain of business media.

The reasons for the growing interest by business media in design can be found in the cross-reference of issues between design and industry at both the macro- and microeconomic levels. The relationship of design to globalism of the marketplace; production and marketing of products in the global context; new patterns of competition; environmental concerns regarding the kinds of products being produced and the way they are manufactured; and changing consumer attitudes, preferences, and habits are the macroeconomic subjects occupying the minds of both business analysts and academicians, and, by transference, the interest of journalists.

On a microeconomic level, writers, consultants, and university economics and business professors are examining individual companies to observe how they are responding to these developments. They have made the design connection at both the macro- and microeconomics level, but the advice they are able to give regarding design is less clear. However, a theme from these observations has emerged: design has to be better managed in corporations.

If, as *Business Week* predicts, design is to be the driving force for business in the 1990s, we'd better get busy and find out how to manage this excellent resource. The alternative is that design can become the misunderstood and mismanaged runaway that finance was in the 1980s or that marketing was in the 1970s.

Designers, educators, and business leaders have the design challenge in their midst now. Some companies are well on their way to mastering design management. Those who haven't will either learn or fall behind in their competitive advantage. It should be sufficient warning that the Japanese government declared 1989 the Year of Design. The hour for mastering the management of design, Tokyo time, is already late.

PART ONE

BRINGING DESIGN INTO THE MANAGEMENT MAINSTREAM

CHAPTER ONE

WHAT IS DESIGN MANAGEMENT?

*Plans get you into things but you got to work
your way out*   WILL ROGERS

WHY IS MANAGING DESIGN DIFFERENT FROM MANAGING ANYTHING ELSE?

I have often wondered if any other discipline devotes as much time to defining itself as design does. Every conference or book about design begins with a discourse about what design is. Nondesigners might assume that this ritual definition exercise is for their enlightenment, but, in fact, the speakers and writers are putting forward definitions as part of an ongoing professional colloquy.

In the early 1980s I began some of my speeches with a brisk list of definitions of design gathered from dictionaries from twenty or so different languages. The point was that the definitions varied rather considerably, emphasizing the uncertainty that exists about what design is and how it should function as an activity.

The definition search continues, but the associated discussions have less to do with niggling over precision of words than with exploring the aspects and scope of design activity and how design can be more effective in its contribution to economic and social goals. In this context the exercise of defining design is worthwhile, and, although many designers experience a certain amount of frustration with the diversity of perspectives about what design is and how the design activity is carried out, the growing number and dimensions of issues identified with the definition process suggest something very positive: Design is dynamic and, by virtue of the scope of its influence, has the potential to become an empowered activity in our society.

Faced with such a rich diversity of perspectives regarding design, my point of view about what design is should be clear at the outset of this book. Though my definition is not as colorful as many that have been offered, it describes what I believe the essence of design to be: *Design is a plan for making a change.* Implicit in this simple definition is the idea that the *plan* is associated with a repository of experiences, observations, information, and skills that are drawn upon by the *designer* to develop an *idea* or *concept. Making* the plan refers to the *activity* of designing and, as this process becomes increasingly more complex, includes the evolution of a *methodology* for the activity of product, communication, or environment creation. The reference to *change* not only engages the concept of *creating something new* but also extends to include ethical considerations of finding *solutions to problems.* Change also requires management of the change process, without which the plan may never be implemented.

DISTINGUISHING BETWEEN DESIGN ACTIVITIES

The result of these design efforts is an object or product, a form of visual communication, or a living or working environment. These tangible results help to distinguish between design activities, providing a codification that is useful in clearing away the thicket of confusion about just what activity is meant when design is being discussed. A kind of design taxonomy, devised by some thoughtful people in the United Kingdom, has become an accepted way to classify design activities. Peter Gorb, former director of the design management program of the London Business School, describes these activities as falling into four broad categories: product design, communications design, environment design, and corporate identity design.[1]

I modify this categorization by distributing corporate identity throughout product, communications, and environment design activities. Corporate identity goes well beyond corporate logos, letterheads, and so forth, which are really communications design. Corporate identity is also rooted in product design and, to a lesser extent, environment design as well as in communications design. Corporate identity is the sum of product design, communications design, and environment design, and the management of all these design elements results in how various constituencies view a company. That view is popularly expressed as the company image. In other words, a company's image is the result of a corporate identity program.

Product Design

The product is the most important thing a company has to say about itself. It is the reason a company is in business. The quality of the products offered by a company will be judged by technical competency, cost, and serviceability. These "hard" values must absolutely be gotten right, since they satisfy the minimum expectations of today's consumers. Competently achieved, these factors bring the competitive positioning up to the starting line. The "soft" values of environmental friendliness, ease-of-use, and distinctive appearance are now recognized as the differentiating values that enable the product to have a competitive advantage.

The product or industrial designer must incorporate all these hard and soft values into the product. This means that the designer must be closely involved in the entire design-to-market stream of activities.

Peter Gorb argues that the value added to a product contributes to gross margin performance, which is a critical measure for all businesses, whether they are the producers of what is sold, the suppliers, the distributors, or retailers.[2] Design contributes to gross margin performance through its influence on a range of management issues that eventually determine product characteristics and gross margin profits. Thus, according to Gorb, design is a pervasive determinate of the profitability performance throughout the chain of activities carried out to produce and sell a product.

The dependency of these segments of the product creation-to-market process on the effectiveness of design is little understood, since the activities of the product designer are most visibly associated with the manufacturer. Even here, design is all too frequently not a highly structured process that is integrated into every phase of management decisions from strategic planning through the design-to-market cycle. In companies where design takes place informally, and often not even considered as design, the result will most likely be inferior product design. No amount of first-rate advertising or corporate identity slickness will make up for substandard product design nor neutralize the negative impact on the stream of research-through-production-to-market activities.

Communications Design

However, a product can successfully combine all the right things but stumble in the marketplace because of the failure to communicate effectively about the product to potential purchasers. Communications design directly supports the product in the marketplace with advertising, promotional materials, packaging, exhibition design, and logo design. Communications design also indirectly supports the product by communicating in a variety of ways to numerous constituencies of the company, relaying messages the company wants to convey about what it makes or the services it provides and how it conducts its business to stockholders; employees and prospective employees; subcontractors and suppliers; news, business, and technical media; government bodies; distributors; and retailers.

Environment Design

The company also sends messages about its concern for quality to its employees, the surrounding community, and all the people who have reasons to visit the company. The environment in which a company's employees work not only has a strong motivational impact on the people upon whom the company depends, it also expresses in a continuous, subliminal way the value the company places upon its employees and the standard of quality that is acceptable. Cleanliness and safety are no longer sufficient work environment goals. Building architecture, showroom design, interior design and layout, furnishings and equipment, signage and visual amenities such as artworks and special landscaping are not just "extras" if the budget allows their inclusion. They are strong elements of corporate identity.

Environment design is also involved with the hard values of capital investment. The buildings, equipment, furnishings, and land are assets representing considerable value to a company. The enhancement of these assets resulting from good architecture and well-designed facilities and equipment makes practical business sense. Maintaining and improving these assets with the continuous consultation of the best architects and designers a company can find is an investment that has both financial and social rewards.

STRUCTURING DESIGN ACTIVITIES FOR SYNERGISTIC IMPACT

The distinction between product, communications, and environment design activities, however, does not mean that they function in splendid isolation from each other. Just as the territorial boundaries between functional activities throughout the corporation are being stripped away, these three areas of design activities should also be highly interactive. Although specific skills are required in each activity, there are both overlapping areas of common skills and possibilities for designers to function in more than one sector. This is a point worth noting, since few corporations have appreciated the positive results that synergy between these areas of activity could generate. It is most common that the communications design activity is a function of marketing. Product design can be either a function of product development and manufacturing or marketing. Environment design is usually managed under a facilities department.

A preferred structural arrangement is for all three activities to be grouped together as the portfolio responsibility of a top-level executive who is at a peer level with senior marketing and technical development executives. This person should report directly to the CEO or, at a minimum, to the executive vice president.

GETTING IT STRAIGHT ABOUT DESIGNERS AND ENGINEERS

There is another aspect of design that causes confusion about who is doing what or even what is meant when referring to design activity. Design in the minds of many people often means engineering design. This is especially true when manufacturing issues or research and technology adaptation to product are discussed. An article in *Business Week,* which presented with some sense of urgency the case for improvements in the United States in concurrent engineering, continuously referred to the design process as engineering design.[3] Clearly, the products and companies cited in the article utilize product designers, and their participation must certainly be significant. Yet design was always referred to as "engineering design."

Ivor Owen, director of the U.K. Design Council and former board director of Thorn EMI, comments, "…I can think of few products that are excluded from a need to think about industrial design. This even includes steam turbines and motors and pumps and a huge range of engineering products. They all need industrial design input. I strongly believe that the schism between engineering design and industrial design has been one of the most damaging issues in manufacturing industry imaginable."[4]

What is the problem here? In short, as Ivor Owen states, it is, in part, the stay-off-my-turf syndrome. The problem is also a straightforward case of misunderstanding the complementary roles of engineering design and industrial design. Each discipline has an important contribution to make, as Figure 1-1 expresses. The fragmentation that exists not only between engineers and designers but between different types of designers is only the tip of the problematic iceberg that impedes the efficiency and effectiveness of the product creation process.

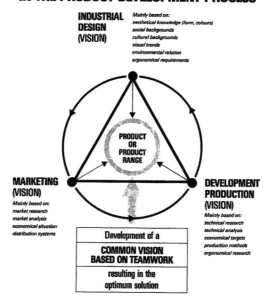

RELATION BETWEEN THE MAIN DISCIPLINES IN THE PRODUCT DEVELOPMENT PROCESS

Figure 1-1. Industrial or product design is an essential part of the product creation process in equal cooperation with engineers and marketers.

The Japanese do not suffer from the problems of "turfism." The interdisciplinary team concept has been developed to a level of sophistication in Japan that goes beyond even the integration of designers, engineers, and marketing people in product creation teams to include social psychologists, anthropologists, and other professional support experts.

American and European companies would benefit from better utilization of the special capabilities of designers to provide "overlap" between disciplines in teaming situations. Good designers can move through overlapping speciality functions because of their training and aesthetic sensibilities. Designers filter ideas through the archives of their experiences and observations; they draw on a general knowledge of technology and materials and ergonomics; they employ visual metaphors in their concepts based on their interpretations of cultural history and social values. Given the freedom to do so, designers are capable of moving beyond the limits of what has already been created to break new ground, to set new boundaries.

In an ideal world, the designer could lead interdisciplinary teams to think about problems in new ways. When asked, "What are the limits of design?" Charles Eames replied, "What are the limits of the problem?"[5] The Japanese have given designers the freedom to push the boundaries of problem constraints. They are coming close to the ideal world every designer dreams about.

Western countries have their work cut out. The integration of design activities into the mainstream of industrial activity must move beyond discussion at design conferences about the isolated, low-status position of design in corporations. The design process is in need of good management.

DESIGN MANAGEMENT AS A NEW DISCIPLINE

If the premise can be accepted that the designer can act as the connector between the variety of activities involved with product creation, then someone and some process must be in place to orchestrate the synergy. Donald E. Peterson, former chairman of Ford Motor Company, says that "the key issue in managing the design process is creating the right relationship between design and all other areas of the corporation."[6] This relationship is not left to chance, in Peterson's opinion, but is structured as an internationally determined and instituted policy of integrating design into the corporate organization. Peterson's experience with the success of the Ford Taurus, which lifted Ford's performance out of the doldrums during his CEO watch and which is well known for its design-driven team approach during development, has convinced him that "the process and the team must be structured so that design, with its innovation oriented input, is equally considered in the trade-offs necessary in any product."

The rationally determined and instituted policy of integrating design into the organizational structure that Peterson endorses is the basic purpose of formalizing design as a managed activity. Design management establishes the fact that a company has design as a program instead of design as an informal activity. Design management makes the existence of design activity visible within the corporate structure and enables design to contribute to strategic planning and to serve as a facilitator for the technical development, production, and marketing processes.

Design management is not merely the assignment of the normal administrative chores to a manager. Budget management, personnel management, and other normal management tasks are part of design management. The distinguishing characteristic of design management is the role it assumes in identifying and communicating ways that design can contribute strategic value to a company. This activity is reinforced with follow-through networking to facilitate the design role in the design-to-market process.

A concise definition of this role and process is as follows: *Design management* is the implementation of *design as a formal program of activity* within a corporation by *communicating the relevance of design* to long-term corporate goals and *coordinating design resources* at all levels of corporate activity to achieve the objectives of the corporation.

Thus, the design manager operates at dual levels. He or she is continuously promoting and identifying the strategic role for design in the corporation while coordinating the day-to-day operational interface with relevant colleagues. The interface with line managers on a continuous basis eventually develops cumulative respect for the contributions designers make to product and communications creation and results in a better understanding of how to deploy design resources more effectively. Situations in which design is ignored or treated as the afterthought or cosmetic tack-on, where overt resistance to design input occurs, or, even worse, where design decisions are made by line managers about matters for which they have insufficient expertise *can* be turned around with good design management. Costly mistakes can be avoided along the entire design-to-market spectrum. Line managers can become supporters and allies, learning to routinely seek designer consultation at the earliest stages of the product creation process.

All these good things presuppose strong design management leadership and a team of capable and creative designers. The actual design work can be that of either an in-house design staff, outside consultant designers, or a combination of both. This is an important subject about which more will be said later.

THE TASKS OF DESIGN MANAGEMENT

To clarify the mistaken notion that design management is primarily applying standard administrative discipline to the design activity and to emphasize that design management functions at both the strategic and operational levels, the tasks of design management are divided into four main spheres of activity:

1. *Contributing to corporate strategic goals.* This design management responsibility includes the development and auditing of a *design policy.* Such a policy establishes design as a formal activity endorsed by top management. Review and audit of a design policy should be ongoing and should involve board- and senior-level management as members of a design policy committee. The design policy specifies the coherent and logical application of design to the way the company creates its products, promotes and supports its products or services, and presents itself to all of its various publics. In short, the design policy is an *articulation of corporate identity.*

Design management should also contribute to *identifying needs.* These needs, which complement both corporate goals and customer satisfaction, are based on a well-developed design and market research program. The design input for identifying needs can supply a critically fresh and important element into spotting trends among competitors before the fait accompli products hit the trade shows. Combining designers' observational skills and general archival knowledge bank with a well-conceived design and market research program (that includes keen observation of competitors' activities and resources) is an aspect of predevelopment that nearly all companies need to emphasize more strongly. Lifestyle research, to be discussed in more detail, is already being practiced by Japanese companies, and designers are central to this new technique for identifying needs.

Note also that designers bring a much-needed perspective from the consumer's point of view. Engineers approach product creation from a perspective of adapting technology to functionability. Making something work is their priority. Marketers are most interested in whether a product will sell. Manufacturers concentrate on cost-efficient production. Designers must satisfy all these objectives, but they are also concerned with whether a product responds to users' needs and wants. They are the consumer's most prominent advocate in the product creation process. As consumers become increasingly more demanding of product safety, environmental friendliness, ease-of-use, and that more elusive quality of specialness that feeds pride of ownership, the designer's consumer advocacy role needs to be more keenly appreciated. The effective identification of these needs is the solid basis on which the course of strategic directions is set. The communication, not only of the identified needs but also of recommendations for the appropriate approach to tailoring a company's response to these needs, is a design management task.

2. *Managing design resources.* This involves recruiting and developing an internal design staff or maintaining close professional contacts in order to hire the most appropriate design consultants to carry out strategic goals. Or, most likely, the design work will be done by a combination of in-house staff and consultants. Giving clear direction to and integrating the efforts of this combination of in-house staff and consultant team is a primary design task.

Providing programs for the renewal of design skills and enlarging the archival information and knowledge base of designers on a subject range from related design activities to social and anthropological sciences to technology innovations is essential to the feeding and nurturing of design talents.

Providing new tools and techniques and training for their use is part of design resource management. Training in new CAD programs, application of ergonomic principles, making available information about new materials, drawing on new design theories, such as semantics and user interface for visual and functional solutions, should all be part of the continuous infusion of resources and information the design manager arranges for the design staff. Assessment of whether consultants are up to the mark in their assimilation of new developments and information is part of the evaluation the design manager should make. In short, the quality of those who do the design work, whether it is executed in-house or by consultants, is a design management responsibility.

3. *Managing the design process.* The much-talked-about imperative for integrating design into the entire product creation process parallels the growing recognition that this process is only efficient as iterative loops of activities rather than as a step-by-step sequence as it has been practiced in the past.

Earl Powell, director of the Design Management Institute, in discussing the companies studied in a collaborative product creation research project with Harvard called TRIAD says,

> Where the design functions—or perhaps better put, the designers and their skills—are well managed, those decisions will create a better, more successful product. It will succeed because it is better designed—more functional, maintainable, manufacturable, and aesthetically pleasing. These many decisions affecting product development are increasingly being made within a structure of collaborative, multidisciplinary teams. In all of the Triad cases, some variety of interdisciplinary teamwork characterized the work from early stages on.[7]

The exact structure and communication process will vary from company to company and, in fact, from project to project within a company. The requisite flexibility demands a commitment to the principle of teamwork and deft but vigilant design management to ensure that as team members change the level of interaction does not erode.

A number of examples of the variations in approach to the principle of interdisciplinary teamwork and how the design process is managed will be described in later chapters.

4. *Cultivating an information and idea network.* Although I can think of few careers whose professionals do not benefit from active contact with peers outside day-to-day work relationships, the design profession absolutely demands it. Design thrives on ideas, and ideas must be nurtured in the cross-fertilization of communications with other designers. Designers outside of one's area of activity. Designers from other countries. Designers from competing companies or consultancies. Designers from other industries. Design critics,

design theorists, design educators. All these people will present a diversity of perspectives that challenges and enlarges the designer's own point of view.

Furthermore, designers need constant exposure to the thinking of other disciplines. They need to be knowledgeable about the world economy and business and market trends on a macroeconomic basis. They need to have access to demographic and social trends and analyses. They should be aware of new business practices and theories. Social and ethical issues are part of their purview. And they should visit major art exhibitions, new architecture, and urban planning sites. All these resources are staples of a balanced diet for the nourishment of ideas and the assimilation of information. They are also essential for making knowledgeable decisions about hiring consultants.

The design manager needs to have a driving curiosity to seek out these reference resources. Companies should support the design manager's efforts to cultivate both the design network and interdisciplinary resources of information and to provide the resources to make these contacts and information sources available to staff designers.

REPEAT: DESIGN MANAGEMENT IS SPECIFIC TO DESIGN ACTIVITY

The brief for managing design should be clear to everyone at all management levels of a company. The only person who can make the brief clear is the senior design manager or director of design in his or her day-to-day interpretations of a design policy. The design policy is a framework for action, not a dead piece of paper brought out for annual "wordsmithing." The strategic goals of the design activity are the substance of a design policy, which reflects both the strategic goals of the company and those that can extend the influence and effectiveness of design. Identifying customer needs, for example, would be a critical and appropriate action goal for a design policy.

Managing the company's design resources is specific to designers' recruitment, upgrading of professional skills, directing of design activity, and provision of state-of-the-art tools and techniques, and career development.

Much continues to be said in business journals about managing product development. The design element, which has too often been the poor cousin in the product creation process (as we shall see in the case studies further on), has a critical contribution to make. Managing the design process as an integral part of an interdisciplinary effort is a major design management task requiring continuous communication, persuasion, negotiation, and initiative-taking to constantly improve the design role in product creation process.

Finally, design management must consciously respond to the challenge of reinforcing the generalist scope of information designers need to carry out their specialist design tasks. Designers have been described as jacks-of-all-trades and specialists in one. The 1990s will demand that the generalist information be related to knowing and caring much more about what consumers are thinking, how they live their lives, and, most important, how they would like to live their lives.

The tasks of design management I have outlined are the essence of managing the design process and resources of a company. But these tasks will be interpreted and carried out in different ways in different companies. What corporations must recognize is that the benefits of a well-managed design program can contribute significantly to their competitive success. This is the starting point on which to build a strong and dynamic design program.

There is also some urgency in making a start in establishing design management as a corporate activity or examining an established corporate design activity for its effectiveness. The competitive pressures are continuing to ratchet up, notch by notch, with each new level introducing more sophisticated, targeted strategies for achieving advantage. Companies are being well warned that the customer of the future is at the top of the corporate hierarchy pyramid, not at the base as was commonly depicted in management diagrams. With the customer at the pinnacle, companies recognizing the connection between design and customers will be the winners of this decade and will be well positioned to enter the next millennium.

REFERENCES

1. Peter Gorb, "What Is Design Management?" Design Management Seminar Papers, London Business School, 1988.

2. Ibid.

3. Otis Port, "A Smarter Way to Manufacture," *Business Week,* April 30, 1990, pp. 64–69.

4. Ivor Owen, "Industry and Design," Design Management Seminar Papers, London Business School, 1989.

5. "Interview with Charles Eames," excerpt reprinted in *Progressive Architecture,* February 1990. Originally appeared in the film, *Design Q&A,* 1972.

6. Donald E. Peterson as quoted by Jeffrey Meikle in "Design in the Contemporary World," Stanford Design Forum, Pentagram Design AG, 1989.

7. Earl Powell, "Designing for Product Success," *TRIAD Design Project Catalogue,* Design Management Institute, Boston, 1989.

CHAPTER TWO

Design: The New Competitive Trump Card

The design dimension is no longer an optional part of marketing and corporate strategy, but should be at their very core

CHRISTOPHER LORENZ,
MANAGEMENT EDITOR
Financial Times

DESIGN MANAGEMENT EMERGES AS A NEW DISCIPLINE

The nature of competition in the fading years of this century has become a subject of almost obsessive examination everywhere in the world. The United States, in particular, is suffering from a crisis of confidence about its ability to create and produce products that can stand head-to-head in competition with west European, Japanese, and, increasingly, other southeast Asian products. Is this business as usual, or is there something fundamentally different about the pressures of competition?

The 1980s ushered in the much-predicted communications era and the turmoil and upheavals associated with dismantling outdated institutions, structures, and practices to make way for new ones appropriate for the information society. This transformation process will continue through the 1990s and into the next millennium, affecting everything from political rule and geographic realignment to economic structures and social patterns of living, learning, and working.

In the economic sector three major developments are challenging the viability of companies everywhere, forcing them to restructure their organizations and devise new strategies for making and selling their products.

The Rise of Globalism

The emergence of the global marketplace has created a new dimension to competition. Products or services that once captured the loyalty of consumers in home markets are now fighting for their lives against challengers from all over the world. To compete even small companies are being forced to venture into markets beyond their national borders. Globalism has dispatched company production centers to the far corners of the world, required new marketing techniques to appeal to diverse cultural customers, and demanded a basic rethinking about what kinds of products companies should be making for this multicultural market.

Regionalism is following hard on the heels of the global phenomenon and is likely to be a dominant development for the rest of this century. The European Community led the regional trend when it conceived of its goal of economic integration by 1992. But, to their dismay, many Europeans found that economic consolidation is difficult to separate from political and social integration. Having only begun to parry and thrust with these issues, the whole of Europe, from the European Free Trade Association (EFTA) countries to the newly independent eastern European countries is pressing for admittance to the EC, raising the uncomfortable specter of a huge regional economic bloc of some 800 million people.

An American regional bloc has emerged with an open trade pact among Canada, Mexico, and the United States. South American countries could join to form a Pan-American union. Southeast Asia will undoubtedly form a Pacific bloc. Japan, Singapore, Taiwan, Hong Kong, and Korea could join with Thailand, The Philippines, Indonesia, and Malaysia, who have already agreed to closer economic cooperation, to create a supranational trading bloc that is rich in natural resources, has pockets of cheap labor, and pursues competitive advantage with iron determination.

The worry is that the regional blocs will create new trade walls. But the national autonomy drive that brought about the splintering of the USSR and Yugoslavia and Czechoslovakia, could result in a world of smaller nation states whose regional bloc membership is overridden by the borderless world of communications and information exchange.

In the global world without borders envisioned by Kenichi Ohmae,[1] people everywhere are empowered by the information communicated fully across borders. People are able to hear and see what is going on all over the world, from political thought to trends in fashion and products.

The global marketplace, already established, in which companies operate in far-flung foreign locations with the full complement of research, design, development, production, and marketing activities, in effect reduces the negative aspects of regional trade bloc barriers. The economic health of Mexico matters to the U.S. company with subsidiary operations there; a Japanese company with production and marketing operations in the United Kingdom has to be concerned about the vitality of the British economy. The network of vested interests of global corporations may counterbalance political decision making in future years.

The Empowered Consumer

The second major development affecting competition is that the empowerment of people all over the world by the flow of communications has changed the profile of the consumer. Consumers with immediate and clear windows to the rest of the world want what everyone else has. In India, for example, the idea of owning the most advanced recorder is a dream to be achieved. And the video-cassette recorder or compact disc player cannot be an outdated piece of equipment designed by Indians using old technology. It must be the newest model. Consumers the world over want what they *know* everyone else has.

The niche markets, or market segmentation, that are the marketing credo of the 1990s have more to do with groups of people by characteristics than by geography. Products will be designed to appeal to adolescents in the 10- to 14-year-old range everywhere in the world; to working women everywhere who want time-saving products; to pensioners with leisure time, good health, and more than adequate spendable money; or to sports enthusiasts (differentiated by the specific sport) in Canada, Spain, or Japan. Such market segmentation by consumer group characteristics is likely to become more and more narrowly defined.

Product Differentiation: Battle Cry of the 1990s

The third competitive issue has to do with new criteria for products growing out of the value shifts of consumers. It is not enough to simply offer functional reliability, competitive price, or even the newest technology. Technological advantage has become vulnerable to the rapid rate at which technology is appropriated by competitors. Producers are also becoming adept at accelerating their new product cycles, reducing speed to market as a factor for competitive advantage.

Differentiation is the buzzword of the 1990s in product competitiveness. But what does this really mean? Will companies simply try to outdo each other with product bells and whistles? The newest challenge is to be able to offer the "soft" values that set a product apart from all the others—the design elements that reduce technical complexity to a simple-to-use product, that clearly offer the promise of making one's job easier or one's leisure time more fun. Or the soft value might appeal to pride of ownership by expressing qualities in the form, materials, or function of the product that are perceived to reflect the user's personal values or characteristics.

Knowledgeable, well-informed consumers of the 1990s will not be acquisitive for the mere sake of ownership as they were in the 1980s. The more sober, socially responsible consumers of the 1990s will expect much more for their money. They will be in the driver's seat, demanding that companies put the focus of their efforts on their customers.

Design is a critical factor in responding to these seminal changes in the consumer and corresponding redefinition of market strategies. Although designers must focus their thinking and responses on technological, economic, and social developments, they must also act on these developments by mediating between the consumer and the manufacturer.

The soft values of product design, which are increasingly becoming the decisive competitive factor for appealing to the more demanding consumer, require design decisions and expertise. The central focus on the consumer in the 1990s means that the product itself must be conceived and designed based on intensive and in-depth study not just of what consumers need or want but of what they could conceivably want. Design is all about anticipation. The designer anticipates new technologies and envisions how they might be translated into useful, easy-to-use, and desired products. The designer also anticipates social changes and identifies new consumer needs and desires as a result of those changes. Designers' intuitive skills, reinforced with information, enable them to make the leap from what exists to what might exist.

With the consumer as the core factor for strategic planning, design has the potential for an influential role in decisions about what a company makes and sells. This contrasts with the past, when the design of products was dictated by what was being made and sold. The focus on the consumer and the product coupled with the designers' anticipatory and intuitive skills leads to the conclusion that designers can be the vital link between the producer and consumer through an expanded role as researchers and product planners. This is a role that has been underappreciated and underutilized by U.S. and European industry. Thus, the global market with its demand for proximity to consumers to research their habits and behavior means that the design function must be dispersed to the key user markets throughout the world.

WAKING UP TO THE IMPORTANCE OF DESIGN

The United States, in particular, has been slow to recognize the importance of design in relation to the developments affecting competitiveness. The role of design has fluctuated over the past six decades. In three periods since the 1930s the practice of design has exhibited distinct emphases as a force of influence in corporations.

In the 1930s the first professional design consultants appeared, led by Raymond Loewy, who has become a symbol of that era. These early visionaries were primarily concerned with *appearance design,* most often referred to as "styling." Their frank and unembarrassed promotion of commercialism, although handled by Loewy and his followers with skill and flair, led eventually to the trivialization of design as a tool of marketing in the postwar period. This situation stubbornly persists in far too many businesses today.

Beginning with the postwar years, however, some designers went well beyond styling and, in fact, abhorred the term and its implications. They included Elliot Noyes, George Nelson, and Charles Eames. These men were at the forefront of the period that introduced the establishment of an integrated *design program* for corporations, which included product, graphic and communications, and architectural design.

The concept of a holistic design program has been successfully adapted by many corporations, including Herman Miller, IBM, Apple, Sony, Esprit, Philips Braun, Bang and Olufsen, to name but a few. Robert H. Hayes, Harvard Business School professor, calls companies such as these world class companies.[2] Hayes describes a world class company as one whose design program goes beyond producing desirable products. These companies, according to Hayes, use design to *facilitate* efficient and simplified manufacturing; to *differentiate* their products from those of their competitors; to *integrate* the concept-to-market process by functioning as a multidisciplinary connector; to *communicate* through visual and written media to their numerous constituencies the values and qualities of their companies.

During the evolution of this second period, stretching from the 1960s to the present, design has become recognized as a strategic competency for corporations rather than merely a service to marketing or engineering. Although this period has been evolving for nearly 40 years, the great majority of companies worldwide, both large and small, are only beginning to be aware of the strategic advantages of an integrated design program. Few understand how to structure it.

The third period overlaps the second and is now in its early stages. It is the *process period*. Those companies that recognize design as a strategic imperative and that have structured design as a program rather than a random activity or several discreet activities are now seeking better ways to manage the design process. Questions are being asked about how to manage the interaction of multidisciplinary product creation teams and the role of the designer within the team. How are staff designers managed so that their unique abilities and qualities are nurtured? When should design consultants be used, and what should their relationship be with in-house designers? Who should be the "design champion," and at what level does this person function in the corporation? How should design research programs be structured to improve the soft-value characteristics of the company's products? In a global organizational structure, how is a decentralized design staff managed? What are the ways design can contribute to the strategic goals of a company? Who implements the concept of a world class design program that integrates all design activities to achieve a true corporate identity?

These are just a few of the questions being raised and discussed during this dynamic period of the development of the design process in corporations. At the heart of the design process exploration is the premise that design is a key strategic tool for the 1990s. But in order for it to be a strategy for corporations, the design process must be managed.

LEARNING MORE FROM JAPAN
THAN HOW TO MANUFACTURE

Stressful competitive pressures for both U.S. and European companies emerged in the 1970s and gathered full force in the 1980s. That competition is commonly referred to as "Japan, Inc.," both because of the perception that the industrial activities of Japan are coordinated and orchestrated as part of a national industrial policy and because this formidable competition seems to extend to every business and service activity in which Japan is involved. No industrial sector in the rest of the world is immune from Japanese competitive challenges.

Until recently attention to the competition situation has been almost entirely focused on issues related to manufacturing and marketing. Automated manufacturing efficiencies, speed of product information, quality superiority (related to defects), homogeneous home market advantage for launching products, subsequent price dumping into export markets, and market share targeting at profit margins unacceptable to Western corporations are some of the issues that have preoccupied U.S. and European companies.

In the last few years attention has begun to be paid to the products themselves. Articles in business magazines and newspapers charged that Western products were not up to the mark against Japanese products. There seemed to be more to the problem than product price and performance. Could it be the design of the products as well? *Time Magazine* and *Business Week* joined *The Wall Street Journal*'s and *Financial Times* of London's lead in reporting on design matters by adding regular design departments to their weekly issues. This growing media interest implied that design literacy on a broad scale needed some sharpening up among both the general population and business managers.

At the same time design conferences and seminars proliferated at the end of the 1980s, often under the sponsorship of governments, business groups, and university graduate business schools. Design management papers at these conferences revealed insights into the importance Japanese industries and the government attach to design. Designers also learned from their design peers in Japan something of how the design process functions and how the prevailing philosophy about design undergirds the product creation process.

The Japanese government's Ministry of International Trade and Industry (MITI) supports the design profession through its ancillary organization, the Japanese Industrial Design Promotion Organization (JIDPO). This official promotional body established the annual G Mark Award in 1957 to raise public awareness of good product design and to motivate industry to raise the design quality level of Japanese products. The G Mark label on products—and now with the program broadened to include transportation and environmental design—has wide public recognition and is a prestige stamp of approval seriously sought by Japanese companies.

JIDPO's active promotion of design achieved a new benchmark in 1989 when, in conjunction with its sponsorship of the biennial International Council of Societies of Industrial Design Congress (ICSID), it expanded this event to become a Japanese Design Year in which design exhibitions, competitions, symposia, and media events were held all over Japan. Nagoya, the host city for the ICSID Congress, chose design as the theme with which to celebrate the 500th anniversary of its founding. A design theme park was constructed, and hundreds of thousands of Japanese flocked to visit it. The government through JIDPO spent $50 million on these design-related events in 1989 alone. Corporations such as Toyota made significant contributions in both funding and other resources. JIDPO worked to maintain the momentum of this interest in design by establishing an international design center in Nagoya.

Japan is not the only Asian country making substantial investments in promoting design as an important component of economic success. Taiwan is matching Japan's annual design promotion expenditure in an ambitious five-year program. The goal of the Taiwanese Trade Ministry, which oversees the effort, is to improve the design quality of the products Taiwan exports. There is also a drive to upgrade the corporate identity of Taiwanese companies to that of world class companies.

Singapore's Trade Development Board sought the advice of Japan's MITI in developing its design promotion program. The Board has sponsored international design symposia, attracting designers and businesspeople from the entire Pacific region. Competitions and exhibitions are mounted as part of the symposium event.

Korea is aggressively developing a design infrastructure with particular emphasis on upgrading its design education programs. The government supports a visiting teacher program and funds overseas study tours for designers. A good designmark competition patterned after the Japanese G Mark was established several years ago.

The focused efforts in design from these serious southeast Asia competitors in the global market makes a strong case for the argument that design as an added value is perceived by these countries as the competitive advantage. With Japan as the leader and role model, it is not likely to be long before the way design functions in Japanese corporations will be emulated by companies in the "Tiger" countries.

SOFT VALUES AS THE FOCUS
OF LIFESTYLE RESEARCH

There is no question that Japan has taken the leadership in defining the soft values that will dominate the consumer buying attitudes of the 1990s. The Japanese are also developing methodologies for researching consumer lifestyles shaped by personal value systems. This "lifestyle research," as it is often called, may well be conducted by Japanese designers in the near future on a global scale.

In an issue of the influential Japanese design magazine *AXIS,* devoted to a "search for concepts in a changing business environment," Motoo Nakanishi, chairman of PAOS Inc., a Japanese design marketing firm, wrote about the shift from uniform consumption patterns to those that defy conventional prediction assumptions.[3] He describes the hierarchy of values to the consumer in goods and services from use value to the value of possession. The value of possession becomes refined to extend to products and services that carry worthwhile information. Once consumers graduate from this stage, they will create a value system of their own, establishing an individualized value system. This era, Nakanishi predicts, will bring an end to economies of scale.

Nakanishi refers to lifestyle research facilities as engaging in a methodology for helping to point the way for corporations to be "creators of value." These "corporate units concerned with research on lifestyle and cultural trends [are] already being carefully groomed and structured to play the role of new kinds of corporate hunter...."[4] The results of this research, conducted both inside and outside a corporation, will eventually permeate the entire corporate culture and marketing strategy, he says.

Exploring the concept of lifestyle research further, the editor of *AXIS,* Yasuko Seki, says, "The search for radically new concepts of marketing and consumption is perhaps the most important issue facing companies as they gear up for informationalization. Consumers are more sophisticated and their interests are widening."[5] Seki describes experimental approaches by Japanese companies for studying consumers and gathering information about new patterns of consumption behavior.

One such research approach, lifestyle research institutes, differs from traditional market research organizations by exploring new directions companies should take and proposing ways for a company to clearly differentiate itself from the competition in its products and through its communications. These lifestyle institutes either are independent companies or operate as an arm of the parent company. In the latter case they are given free reign, relieved from budget and planning constraints, to pursue broad perspectives for future company strategies.

Antenna shops are another Japanese design research approach. These may look like the usual retail store, but they actually function as laboratories for testing new product ideas and fresh ways to establish relationships with consumers. Such shops may be sponsored by a company and yet carry other companies' products in order to gain insight into realistic marketplace perceptions and situations.

Urban design studios, which are an integral part of a company's design organization, are another variation in the search for ways to get close to customers. These design "inposts" are meant to absorb the pace and pulse of city life as the crucible of trend setting. Because many corporations are now situated away from urban centers and are in fact now the "outposts" of activity, urban design studios represent an acknowledgment that corporate isolation from the centers of cultural gravity must be redressed.

Designers occupy central roles in the operation of all three examples of these new lifestyle research approaches. This is because, as Nakanishi notes, "the information obtained and hypotheses built up through research into lifestyle and cultural trends must eventually come to fruition in concert with new design activity."[6] Only design that creates value, he adds, that is, design created within the framework of corporate marketing, can be capital efficient.

The pioneering of these experimental research programs is in stark contrast to the normal pattern in most Western companies in which designers often react to a design brief prepared by marketers and engineers. The dominant participation of Japanese designers in the research and product planning stages reveals much about the structure and process of design in Japanese corporations.

Kiyoshi Sakashita has described the design organization he heads for Sharp at various design conferences as consisting of over 200 people working in the Corporate Design Center. He says that the four design centers at their main factories in Japan and additional seven design groups spread throughout the United States, Europe, and Tokyo are managed in every aspect from planning and strategy to finance by the Corporate Design Center. Because Sakashita is a member of the Sharp board of directors, his influence as a designer is imprinted on the entire spectrum of the company's business activities.

Aki Amanuma, formerly general manager for Sony's Global Industrial Design Center, in a paper delivered at the *Financial Times* Conference in London in October 1990 on the theme "Product Strategies for the 1990s," noted that the Sony Design Center is part of the Merchandising and Product Communication Strategy Group.[7] That complicated designation can be simplified to qualify as a perfect example of Robert Hayes's world class corporation in which design, marketing, and corporate communications function together as a single unit.

Amanuma describes the role of design within this group as "a kind of coordination work between each unit. This horizontal structure is very important to keep consistency of our design and to create crossover products such as audio visual products." He also gave an impression of a great deal of freedom of territory for Sony designers by describing job assignments as flexible. "The designer tries to do a marketing job or to create the ad strategy. Marketing people cannot be designers but a designer can be a marketer." He spoke of a mixture of top-down and bottom-up decision making, contending that this flexibility, with the discussions and arguments created by bottom-up participation and top-down decisions, "improve everyone's concentration" and is key to the product development and design operation at Sony.

What says it all in terms of the importance Japanese companies place on design is the amount of financial resources they devote to design. According to JIDPO research, as reported by Arnold Wasserman at the same *Financial Times* Conference in 1990, the leading Japanese companies spend between 4 and 6 percent of total R&D for design. This compares to between 0.5 and 1.5 percent invested by U.S. and European companies on professional product design. A few U.S. companies spend up to 4 percent on consumer product design. Wasserman commented, "It tends to be a surprise to business executives that they have to pay for design. Since design is not in the MBA course syllabus, they don't think it is necessary to allocate resources to it. American business executives, in particular, treat design as an automatic outcome of the product development process, not as a discrete business function requiring planning and management."[8]

The contrast between Japan and the U.S. business executives in their focus on long-term horizons is strikingly evident in this attitude about investment in design. A design program that is embedded in the strategic thinking of a company cannot be turned on and off to conform to the fortunes or misfortunes of the profit-loss statement. The early 1990s recession in the United States demonstrated that design is still considered a random and therefore an expendable activity in tough times. The design profession experienced a true economic depression as company design staffs were slashed and many consultancies struggled to survive. The International Design Conference at Aspen was moved to reflect the dismal situation with a conference in 1991 called "Bare Bones" and, in 1992, "Get Real!" The plight of designers telegraphed the message that for all the talk about product competitiveness, the point was being missed. Companies "just didn't get it." A design program is a development investment that can only produce effective results if it is sustained over a long period. This kind of long-horizon attitude is more likely to take root in industry with the endorsement and gentle but persistent prodding of the government.

GOVERNMENT COMMITMENT TO DESIGN IN OTHER COUNTRIES

When the first Japanese ICSID Congress was held in Kyoto in 1973, the conferees could have dismissed as professional preening the declaration of their Japanese hosts that Japan would move from an export-based nation to a design-based nation. The seriousness with which government and industry have addressed their design capabilities since that time indicates that this was not an idle boast. It has become a national and industrial strategy. The design-based profile of Japan means that its exports will be all the more formidable competition for other countries.

In Europe a number of governments also give significant support to design. France's Ministry of Culture, through two subsidiary organizations—the Agence pour la Promotion de la Création Industrielle and the Centre de Création Industrielle (based at Centre Pompidou)—foster links between designers and industry by sponsoring design exhibitions and cosponsoring competitions with industry. The Ministry of Industry also supports design with the sponsorship of 10 regional design centers. A school of design, the Ecole Nationale Supérieure de Création Industrielle, was established under government aegis in 1982.

Spain has been aggressively promoting its design capability as a partner for successful export of products and fashions. Four regional design centers are working hard to forge connections with Spanish industrialists and help establish a design education infrastructure.

The Scandinavian countries have a long history of government support for design. Government-sponsored design centers are the pivot points for design advocacy with industry, the general public, and education institutions. Finland, contending with an anguishing economic readjustment, is up and running with the first design management academic program on the continent. The University of Industrial Arts Helsinki (UIAH) conducts a graduate-level program called "Design Leadership," drawing on an international guest faculty to teach design management course segments.

Design in Germany, in particular, in what was formerly West Germany, is supported by the regional governments. In Baden-Würtemburg, for example, a design center has been established in Stuttgart to work closely with that state's Ministry for Economic Affairs. As in the majority of government-sponsored design programs, industrial competitiveness is considered the rallying point for design support. The Stuttgart Design Center, with the blessings of the Ministry for Economic Affairs, sponsors a biennial design competition in which products from any place in the world are eligible for consideration. The most innovative, thoughtfully designed, and excellently executed products are selected by an international jury to represent the highest level of state-of-the-art product design. The point is to raise the consciousness of industry and the public in general to the importance of design quality for both producers and users. Such design awareness programs seem to be effective. According to a report by *Design Magazine,* two-thirds of the German population over 14 years old understand design to be the design of basic commodities.[9] Twenty-seven years ago a similar poll revealed that only 27 percent of the German population had any idea what design really meant.

Government enthusiasm for design in the United Kingdom was a model for other countries during the 1970s and 1980s. Far-ranging, ambitious programs were funded by the Thatcher government to attack the problem of design awareness from every angle. Design education programs were established in schools at all age levels; advanced design education was supported to train design professionals, turning out, arguably, the best trained designers in the world. Design advisory services were established to assist small and medium-sized businesses to make appropriate design consultant connections. The Design Council presided over this yeasty mixture of design affairs and also operated the highly visible Design Center in London, which attracted steady streams of the public to its exhibitions and design information services.

In spite of all these efforts, the government and business observers could make few claims for the successful application of design, which, in turn, should have improved Britain's export position abroad. British industrialists, the government complained, seemed impervious to absorbing the lessons of design that had been so energetically presented. Although a commitment to design has not been abandoned by the government, alternative approaches to its promotion are being tested. One of these is to target specific export industries in which design is crucial, primarily in the consumer goods sectors, rather than the all-inclusive blanketing of industries such as the engineering-driven industrial equipment sector. This more selective approach for design support sets the government direction for the 1990s. Public education programs are also being scaled down in favor of concentrating efforts on target industries.

In the United States, with the exception of small grants from the National Endowment for the Arts for specific projects, the government has paid scant attention to design. The United States was until only recently the major exception to having a national design center or government-sponsored design council. Now, however, a number of developments by professional design societies, educational institutions, and design-related organizations point to a more assertive, self-help posture for design advocacy. The American Center for Design in Chicago (formerly the Society of Typographic Arts) declared its goal to promote excellence in design education and practice and to serve as a national information center for design and its role in U.S. culture and economy. The Cooper Hewitt Museum in New York, part of the Smithsonian Museum group, is increasingly assuming the role of a U.S. design museum. And in early 1991 the American Design Council was formed to bring together under an umbrella organization all design-related groups.

These actions to coordinate activities and information will undoubtedly give more force to design advocacy and assist the individual efforts of colleges and universities in their recent interest in exploring ways to build a research base for design and for devising new approaches to teaching.

These are important initiatives, but they would be strengthened if the government would recognize the relationship between design and competitiveness as so many other countries' governments do. Even more important than financial support is the influence that government interest in the subject would have on keeping design as an issue alive in the public debate about industrial competitiveness.

CONCENTRATING THE MINDS OF BUSINESS EXECUTIVES ON DESIGN

Media advocacy for design, coupled with the implications of the added-value imperatives for achieving competitive advantage have placed the topic of bolstering corporation design performance on the agendas of business conferences. These conferences are being sponsored all over the world by governments, academic institutions, business publications, and professional design organizations. Although much of the content of these events is devoted to raising the awareness of design as a strategic business activity, the main thrust is to position design in the context of process and how this process can be managed to reap the advantages being captured by world class companies.

In 1989 the Design Management Institute (Boston), a pioneer organization in its advocacy for design management and in its sponsorship of excellent programs in pursuit of knowledge and information exchange about the design process in corporations, joined with the Harvard Business School in the organization and sponsorship of a major design management project. Named TRIAD to denote the global aspect of both the representation of the companies involved in the project and the arena in which they operate, the project approached the subject of design management with a cluster of information-effective activities. An exhibit was mounted, which combined text, visual displays, and models, to present case studies of 13 global companies in which design was used as a strategy to achieve competitive advantage. An accompanying catalogue detailed the design process in each case study and how it was managed. The exhibition opening was kicked off with a seminar for business managers jointly conducted by DMI and Harvard. DMI arranged an intensive travel schedule for the exhibition, sending it throughout the United States, Europe, and southeast Asia (the TRIAD regions). Exhibition-sponsoring organizations organized local events to boost both interest in the exhibit and to extend the dialogue on the subject of design management. In London, for example, the *Financial Times* sponsored a two-day conference, "Product Strategies for the '90s," which attracted several hundred participants, and the Design Center, which sponsored the exhibition, hosted an opening reception.

In the foreword to the catalogue accompanying the TRIAD exhibition, which is entitled "Designing for Product Success," John H. McArthur, Dean of the Harvard Business School says,

> As global competition becomes more intense, new dimensions of competitive strategy have received increasing attention. One of the most important is design and the management of design. Even as recently as five years ago, most managers considered good design almost frivolous. They viewed designers as people who simply determine the color and overall appearance of design.
>
> When the success of companies like Braun in Germany or Sony in Japan is analyzed, however, the significance of design to their company's reputation and profitability becomes clear. Design—from reliable performance to quality appearance—is indeed a crucial competitive weapon.[10]

The TRIAD project is but one example of the serious attention being paid to the topic of design management. Design advocates, it seems, have finally realized that abstract discourses about design fail to elicit interest from pragmatic businesspeople. But when discussions focus on questions of how the design process can be integrated into strategic planning and the functional and operating processes of a company so that design can make an effective contribution to a company's competitive position, businesspeople begin to listen.

The clues regarding design ascendancy are there for everyone to see in the importance Japanese industry is placing on soft values in their goods and services, which, purely and simply, are the purview of design research, planning, and execution. Taking this emphasis to the next dimension, the management of the design process for the effective implementation of design points to the new skill to be mastered in the 1990s: design management.

REFERENCES

1. Arnold Wasserman, "Learning from Experience—An Approach to Design Strategies for Product," paper delivered at the *Financial Times* International Conference, London, 1990.

2. Robert H. Hayes, "Managing Design for Strategic Impact," paper delivered at the Second International Design Forum, Singapore, 1990.

3. Motoo Nakanishi, "Design and Lifestyle Research in the Information Age," *AXIS* Excerpts, vol. 31, Spring 1989, pp. 12–13.

4. Ibid.

5. Yasuko Seki, "Search for Concepts Is On," *AXIS* Excerpts, vol. 31, Spring 1989, pp. 5–6.

6. Motoo Nakanishi, "Design and Lifestyle Research in the Information Age," *AXIS* Excerpts, vol. 31, Spring 1989, p. 13.

7. Aki Amanuma, "Industrial Design as a Source of New Product Ideas," paper delivered at the *Financial Times* International Conference, London, 1990.

8. Arnold Wasserman, "Learning from Experience—An Approach to Design Strategies for Product," paper delivered at the *Financial Times* International Conference, London, 1990.

9. "Design and the State," *Design Magazine,* London, March 1990.

10. John H. McArthur, Foreword, "Designing for Product Success," essays and case studies from the TRIAD design project exhibit, Design Management Institute, Boston, 1989.

CHAPTER THREE

Ten Design Management Issues and How They Connect to Corporate Strategy

We look forward to the time when design
management is not taken for granted, but is
properly regarded as both an essential
dimension of competitive strategy and an
integral part of managerial education
DEAN JOHN H. McARTHUR
HARVARD BUSINESS SCHOOL

Driven by the realities and challenges of the global economy that emerged during the 1980s, corporations are finally recognizing design as a key contributor to gaining competitive advantage. The 1990s will also see an overlay of new imperatives for solving environmental and social needs added to competitive pressures. Designers, because of their traditional concerns for humane solutions to industrial and societal problems, and a zest for problems that require fresh, unorthodox solutions, have an opportunity to provide invaluable leadership to business and industry in these uncharted waters.

However, although awareness of the important role design can play in the corporation has risen, design is still underutilized as a strategic tool in all but a few corporations. Commitment to a *design program* that is entrenched in the company's strategic and operational thinking and practices requires *management of the design process.* Design management is still in the early development stages as both a skill and technique for achieving corporate goals. Educators, designers, and corporations need to work together to give substance and structure to the design management process and develop the resources required to establish design management as an authoritative and integrated part of the corporate structure.

Understanding the important issues related to design management is a way to begin to address the development of this new management resource. The number and scope of issues grows at every forum where design management is discussed. In preparation for the 1990 annual conference of the Industrial Design Society of America (IDSA), which had design management as its subject theme, designers submitted 153 issues they wanted addressed at the conference. Students at Northwestern University attempted to tackle several hundred design management issues in a project study. Since a basic law of management is to reduce a problem to its essential elements, I have culled a manageable, focused group of 10 issues based on my own design management experience and drawn from discussions in which I have participated in recent years in international forums about design management. At the end of this chapter, I have provided a list of questions to help you determine where your company stands on these key issues. These key design management issues follow.

1. THE STATUS OF DESIGN IN CORPORATIONS

Much has been made of the importance of a "design champion" in a corporation, usually a CEO, who, by virtue of her or his top position, decrees to the company hierarchy that design will be treated respectfully as an essential part of corporate business activities. Container Corporation, CBS, IBM, Herman Miller, Apple, Sony, Olivetti, and Philips are frequently cited as examples of prestigious companies whose presidents were dedicated advocates for design in their corporations. The flaw in this conventional design champion wisdom is that after the CEO/design advocate passes from the scene, the commitment of the company as a whole has a tendency to fade. Unless design is established as an integrated and managed process that is clearly appreciated for its contribution to corporate goals, the force of a single, influential personality will be as ephemeral as the dew drop on a rosebud. The leadership of a design program should depend on a structured, permanent design manager position. The status of that person, the director of design, in the corporate structure should be on a peer level with senior managers in marketing, manufacturing, research, and finance, and the director of design should report directly to the president, CEO, or executive vice president.

Within the corporate design organization itself, designers should also be operating on an equal level of authority and compensation with their peers in engineering, production, and marketing. Designers have not traditionally been accepted at such levels, which has had a negative impact on the quality of design talent a company can attract and keep. The status of designers in corporations also influences the numbers and quality of young people entering design studies. This point is of crucial importance to the question of whether the design profession can deliver on the building expectations by industry of design.

The overarching issue of the status of design in the corporation affects every aspect of a design program: how fully it is integrated into the research-to-market stream; the quality of design talent; the leadership capabilities designers can give to innovation; the force with which design can influence the quality of all activities of the corporation.

2. DESIGN AS A STRATEGIC FACTOR FOR ACHIEVING CORPORATE GOALS

With the leveling of basic product factors—cost, technology, function—to the minimum acceptable criteria for competitiveness, design is the element that can endow products with qualities that separate them from their competitors. Design will increasingly be the added value that makes a competitive difference.

As companies continue to enter international markets, they will depend on designers to create global products by designing to the broad specifications of international requirements for technical standards and safety and environmental regulations. But more will be demanded of designers to appeal to the narrower definitions of consumer preference based on demographic characteristics and, for some products, cultural differences. Designer expertise will be called upon to design basic product chassis or "envelopes" to which numerous variations can be tailored. The design approach will be toward system design.

Designers are uniquely qualified to be the connector between the end user and the marketing and engineering people. The designer's training makes him or her the most selectively observant eyes the company can have to track the clues that lead to assessments about trends in lifestyles and changes in social priorities. From these observations, designers have the ability to make the intuitive leap to imagine what consumers need, want, or may enthusiastically accept as a new product. Unlike marketers, designers can translate this research information into appropriate product designs.

It is fair to assume that design can effectively deliver not only on competitive grounds but also by satisfying growing consumer demand for products that are environmentally benign in their use of materials, energy usage, disposability, and efficiency of operation. In fact, environmental and social characteristics of products may be the most compelling competitive advantage of the 1990s and consequently a top strategic goal into the next century.

The corporation is likely to come under strong scrutiny in the 1990s from shareholders and consumers for both its profitability and social responsibility. Designers can play a vital strategic role in giving direction to and management of the concrete activities that comprise a corporate identity. Listen carefully to your designers in these matters!

3. EXPANDING THE SCOPE OF DESIGN WORK

Designers will only be able to contribute significantly to the strategic goals of a corporation if their unique combination of specialist and generalist capabilities are put to work in areas beyond the mostly limited "styling" activities still prevalently associated with design work. In one of the periodic design reviews presented to members of the Philips Board of Management, a young personal computer designer was giving a spirited explanation of his role in the product creation process for a personal computer called "Pronto." One of the board members, whose area of responsibility was manufacturing, expressed astonishment that the young designer was involved in engineering decisions. "What does this have to do with design?" he asked. The deputy design director, Frans van der Put, replied that it had everything to do with design! He explained that as products such as computers are becoming more and more technically complex, it is the designer's job to reduce that complexity to an understandable and enjoyable relationship between the machine and the user. Since such products have more to do with "thinking" than "doing," interaction design is an absolute priority that requires a team of people trained and experienced in interface design, graphic design, industrial design, and software engineering. The team of designers is concerned with the users and how they will react with the product and will work from that point toward the technical function and the constraints or possibilities involved. The engineer begins with the technical function and works toward the more subjective, user-reaction concerns of the designers. It is pretty clear, van der Put concluded, that the form of technically complex products, although important, is being overtaken as a design concern by user interface design.

If one can accept design critic Ralph Caplan's premise that designers approach a product design problem from the outside-in and engineers work from the inside-out, it is clear that designers are asking at the outset broad questions about product users.[1]

Who will use the product? How will they use it? How will it be sold to potential users? How does this product fit into the current product range of the company? How does it stack up with competitors' products? What is its potential for spawning future product generations? (Now the designer is moving inside the product.) Will it be easy and safe for the consumer to use (further inward to meet and influence the engineer)?

In an ideal product creation process, designers participate with product managers in the brief-writing stage and even earlier, working with top management in strategic planning discussions, with marketing managers in research, and with engineers and product managers in the development stages.

Philip Kotler, in his opening remarks at a conference organized by Northwestern University's International Business Development units in 1989, acknowledged that new, vital criteria for competitiveness was the added value of appropriateness and fit to lifestyles and to resource availabilities, conservation, and environmental protection requirements. These additional design-driven characteristics help to illuminate how design can make a contribution to competitive advantage. But Kotler noted they still leave us lacking the full answer about the potential scope for design. He wondered if design was being sufficiently employed to make appropriate use of available or acquirable technology by avoiding early obsolescence and instead setting up the potential for successive generations of new or improved technologies. Product designs, he said, should also be evaluated for how well they fit into the most likely distribution, storage, sales, and other systems of which they are destined to be a part. Kotler acknowledged that answering these questions, which are critical determinants of "good design," is not easy. It means reaching into the design process itself to learn the extent to which these matters can be more effectively considered and mastered.[2]

Clearly, the scope of design in the minds of people such as Kotler, John McArthur, Robert Hayes, and other business experts who are examining its role in industry exceeds that which even many designers have considered. The sphere of activity and influence of design management, as a result, may be far broader than has been envisioned.

4. FULL INTEGRATION OF DESIGN IN THE PRODUCT CREATION PROCESS

The division of tasks and turf battles of earlier decades were recognized in the 1980s as a major obstacle to innovation, quality achievement, and reduction of development-to-market time in U.S. and European industries. The serial product development process, it was understood, had to be replaced by the parallel process. The reality is that this very rational concept is easier postulated than carried out, striking as it does at the heart of the Western world's cherished concept of territorial domain. Design, as the group so often and so long operating in the shadow of engineers and marketers, is still, according to testimony by designers, fighting for admission to the product creation process on a peer level.

Corporations need to address this issue by specifically developing a process and procedures for achieving product creation integration.

5. DESIGN-LED INNOVATION AS STIMULUS TO PRODUCT CREATION

The design function, in my experience, has a much better chance of achieving integration parity with its engineering and marketing partners in the product creation process if it earns its credibility by taking the initiative when it has the opportunity to do so, or better, *makes* its own opportunities. Designers have no difficulty generating ideas. That's what they do. Good designers conceive ideas that often leap into unknown territory of the new, the untried, the untested. They are able to make large shifts away from conventional thinking. Talented designers can arrive at such paradigm shifts by drawing on the archives of their personal experience—experience that is based on practice, visual observation, and multisourced information.

However, it is not enough to merely generate innovative ideas, even good ideas. All designers, and even more than a few marketers and engineers, can tell anecdotes about the good ideas that never made it off the drawing board. It has to be acknowledged that practical considerations of cost, production capabilities, macroeconomic conditions, where valid—and proven validity is, or course, the pivot point of controversy—may justify the consignment of a good design idea to the concept graveyard.

But more often, a good design idea fails to be developed because it has not been vigorously and effectively explained, promoted, and even fought for. This is an important task of design management. The design manager should operate on a daily basis as the impresario for the ideas generated by the design staff or consultants. *All* designers will experience a higher rate of success for the development of their design ideas if they are as verbally skillful as they are visually talented.

When an innovative design idea is conceived on the initiative of designers and leads the company in a direction that contributes to achieving its strategic goals, the design-led innovation greatly strengthens the product creation process. As part of the integrated team of players in product creation, designers have much more to offer than simply to function as reactors to briefs from marketing.

6. MANAGEMENT OF CORPORATE DESIGN RESOURCES

The human resources and financial capital of a company that are brought to bear to produce design output must be responsibly, skillfully, and creatively managed. All these activities together contribute to the corporate identity of a company. A synergistic approach to design management involves, at a minimum, the following tasks:

1. *Human resource management:*   recruiting design staff personnel; providing career growth opportunities for designers; developing renewal training and broad exposure opportunities; providing access to research information across a broad spectrum of disciplines; developing and monitoring a design policy; creating a clear organizational structure; hiring and directing consultants for specified tasks.

2. *Capital resource management:*   acquiring state-of-the-art design tools and aids; exerting an influence on the quality of the buildings and grounds that comprise the company's capital investment and affect employees' work environment.

3. *Financial resource management:*   developing and managing the design operating and research budget.

4. *Corporate identity management:*   acting as liaison between product design and communications support services such as advertising, public relations, special promotion, exhibitions; developing and managing the house style program.

Recalling the definition of design management, managing corporate design resources is one-half of the design management mandate. The other half—communicating the relevance of design to long-term corporate goals—is the charter for converting corporate design resources from passive assets into active, contributory elements of corporate strategy. A relative handful of companies have an understanding of the value of managing the synergy between product design, communications, and capital assets to achieve the much-sought-after, high-quality corporate image. Those who have understood the high impact of a well-coordinated program, such as IBM, Herman Miller, Apple, and Sony, have benefited handsomely by adhering to this principle.

7. MANAGING A GLOBAL DESIGN ORGANIZATION

Few companies, even small ones, will fail to be touched by globalism of the marketplace. Companies choosing not to stray into foreign territories will find that they will be forced to confront foreign competitors anyway—in their home market. The increasing internationalism of business means that organizational restructuring will be necessary to deal with questions of where to produce, what kind of products to produce, how to market and distribute them. Many companies have already experimented with new structures, and most will agree that there is no magic formula for doing it right.

The conventional wisdom is that decentralization is basic to the management of a global business. The rapid changes in economic conditions, trade conditions, and world events require the agility that can come only with a flexible, close-to-the-market cluster of business activities. Research, design, development, production, marketing, distribution, and service must be dispersed to key world market locations, with broad policy matters and coordination roles orchestrated at company headquarters.

Successful management of the decentralized corporation raises challenges. For design management, key issues center around how to maintain a consistent design image; how to keep small dispersed groups of designers from becoming dominated by their marketing and production associates; how to maintain effective communication to keep the valuable flow of ideas between designers going.

8. DESIGN AS A FORCE FOR QUALITY

In the 1980s the United States set about relearning quality principles from the Japanese, who learned about quality in the first place from the United States after World War II. But as Jeffrey Meikle points out in "Design and the Contemporary World," a design commentary and publication of the proceedings of the Stanford Design Forum in 1988, W. Edwards Deming and J. M. Juran, the quality gurus, focus not on the quality of the design of a product but on the quality of workmanship and functional reliability.[3] Articles about quality in scholarly and business magazines are almost totally directed to the manufacturing process. But Meikle comments, "A corporation might succeed in reaching that near mystical goal of `zero defects' without ever actually attaining quality—if a product happens to be poorly designed from the start."

My own experience from my years at Herman Miller, where the high standards set by design *demanded* nothing less than quality production, demonstrated to me that not only are design and production integrally bound but that, in fact, good design can be the force for quality manufacturing.

This simple proposition, which the Japanese figured out, apparently without the help of Deming and Juran, was brought home to me again in a reverse way when I was a speaker at an International Quality Conference in Dublin. The organizers and conferees were absolutely astounded that the subject of design was on the agenda. It was a first-ever presentation about the relationship between quality and design. This notion caused a buzz of interest—such a revolutionary concept!

Of course, it should be understood in the context of this issue, and, in fact, throughout this book, that just because design is consciously employed or because a company engages in a design program does not necessarily guarantee that the design results are good. Who makes the judgment about the quality of design? This is, in my opinion, the thorniest of all design management issues.

9. WHO SHOULD BE A DESIGN MANAGER?

Who should be a design manager is an issue about which there is wide disagreement among those in design-related fields, and businesspeople and educators also see this issue in very different ways. Business managers with whom I have worked at both Philips and Herman Miller come down on the side of a design-trained professional with experience in both design and management of the design process. Perhaps surprisingly, that position is more strongly taken at

Philips, where the suggestion is dismissed that a business manager could be an acceptable managing director of design. There is for the most part the belief at Philips that, although a design manager should possess both generalist and specialist (design) skills and experience and can cross discipline borders with confidence, nondesign managers cannot make authoritative design decisions; of course, in the day-to-day fray, this belief is sometimes conveniently forgotten.

At Herman Miller in recent years nondesigners have been given the responsibility for design management with uneven results. This direction is perhaps due to the strong role of design that is deeply embedded in the company culture. As a result, everyone "owns" the design role. Design jargon flourishes at Herman Miller. Everyone knows the phrases of design-speak. But a superficial understanding of design does not replace lifelong professional design experience.

It has been my experience in many different situations in both companies that when difficult decisions about design have to be made, it comes down to a matter of judgment. Those judgments are ideally based on the cumulative layering of design education, which may include studies in architecture and art, with an obsessive lifelong learning in these fields. Study and learning is interwoven with experience in design practice and investigation into new design tools and techniques; product design and development; production processes; new materials technologies; ergonomics; computer-aided design and other design tools. Added to these is an abiding interest in marketing, macroeconomics, the social sciences, advertising, and all forms of graphic communications. In addition, the judgment call is informed by assiduous monitoring of design achievements, developments and critical analysis in product design, architecture, graphic design, fashion design, and interior design. Making the connections between all these cross-disciplinary influences is the daily thought process of the designer—the reservoir of information from which design decisions are drawn.

It is my observation that there is proportionately the potential for as many good managers among designers as there is in any other field. It was quite gratifying at Philips Corporate Industrial Design (CID) to note how many designers performed management tasks with competence and creativity. They had been given the *opportunity* to be managers. And they were provided a clearly developed structure in which to perform their management functions. There are also a sufficiently large number of design consultancies with millions of dollars of annual billings to demonstrate that designers can manage successful businesses.

Yet the perception of designers as befuddled managers exists. The president of one of America's largest corporations admitted at a design forum that, although he champions design as a corporate strategy, he could not imagine a designer ever becoming president of a sizable corporation. This perception probably owes more to stereotype rather than proven capabilities. This bias also reflects a lack of understanding about designers and how they work.

The design skill of synthesizing information, observation, and experience offers valuable possibilities for developing creative and effective management skills of the sort that are badly needed today in Western countries. Peter Gorb based his London Business School design program on the premise that if business managers can be taught some basic design skills, they would be far more proactive in their management style. The traditional graduate business school case study method, he contends, has entrenched an approach that tends to emphasize the analytical decision-making process rather than pursuing the action necessary to solve the problem.

Gorb says the point is not to train business students to be designers but to help them manage better by practicing the methodology of the designer in dealing with problems. In addition to teaching the hands-on problem-solving process used by designers, Gorb's design management program promotes a heightened level of visual literacy, which he believes would help business managers deal more confidently and sensitively with all the artifacts that surround them in their business world. These artifacts include not just the things they make but the things they use every day in the conduct of their business affairs.[4]

This is a powerful argument with broad implications for the tightening competitive crunch Western companies will be experiencing from the Japanese. The more visually literate, artifact-appreciative Japanese are having no difficulty understanding the case for the design value that will differentiate products in the coming years. Gorb's theory of visual literacy and artifact appreciation may also help explain why Japanese managers are more adroit in adopting the synthesis, activist approach to decision making and have more respect for the contribution of their designers.

It should follow that if business managers would benefit from acquiring some of the skills of the designer, designers themselves by virtue of their education and experience ought to have the potential to be very good managers indeed. It should be no more unreasonable to assume that designers could learn standard management theories and skills as an extension of their design education than to accept the idea that business students can learn the synthesis and observational skills of designers.

What is really being argued here is that designers and business managers can learn a great deal from each other. The design manager, as a respected part of the management team and a *designer by training and experience,* can make a valuable contribution both in holding the company to a high standard of visual literacy and in serving as an antidote to the analytical, financially focused thinking that is typical of management school graduates. The exhortations of economists and business journalists flooding the pages of their books and magazine articles, which urge industrialists to put the customer at the center of their thinking certainly has to do with caring about artifacts, since these are what one supplies to customers.

Designers have always cared first and foremost about customers and the artifacts they design for them. It would be one of the most ironic of lost opportunities if, at this time, when interest in design management is surging, business managers should co-opt the design manager role, leaving designers in the position of lesser authority to promote and implement their ideas.

10. DEVELOPING DESIGN MANAGEMENT TRAINING RESOURCES

The interest in design management and the reasons it has become a focus of discussion among designers, educators, and corporations have been discussed in earlier sections. The issue now is not so much whether design management should be formalized as an education discipline as *how* the curricula should be developed. Universities and graduate business schools in the United States and Europe are grappling with this question.

I see a bigger issue looming that begs for broader discussion: For whom are these design management programs being developed? There is a strong tendency to direct them to business students on the grounds that if business managers had a better understanding of design, they would make far better use of it as a strategic resource. I do not disagree with the idea that the more people who are sensitized to making good use of design, the more opportunities there will be for design to make effective contributions to business activities and achieve corporate strategic goals. What I am concerned about as countless universities develop design management programs is that these may be directed to business students and not to designers. If this tendency continues, the design profession is in danger of becoming degraded in its stature and further removed from the decision-making centers of gravity in corporations. As a consequence, the profession will lose bright young people who would only be attracted to design if it were seen as offering opportunities for management positions of stature in corporations. One can easily imagine a retinue of business-educated design management graduates ready to take the reins of authority for design decisions. But where are the talented designers who will feed them the creative new ideas? Only those designers who are content to live their professional lives under the thumb of nondesigner managers will be available to provide design input. Such designers will not contribute design leadership but will merely carry out the marketing and engineering interpretations of how a product should be designed. This puts corporations right back where they started, with all the problems of a low-status, nonintegrated design component.

More attention needs to be paid to consideration of the desirable skills, interests, and personal characteristics of a design manager. If there can be some consensus about the qualities a design manager should possess, it might become more clear that design management development should not only *not* exclude designers but should be specifically designed to build on their education and experience.

There should be closer dialogue between educators, designers, and corporations about the desirable goals of design management programs, including who these should be directed to and what the appropriate curricula should be to achieve the goals.

The ten issues discussed here form the basis for analysis and discussion about this emerging new management and design discipline. Part 2 focuses on these issues by first describing the design programs of two very different corporations and then by presenting specific design case studies demonstrating how these refer to the design management issues.

REFERENCES

1. Ralph Caplan, *By Design,* St. Martin's Press, New York, 1982, pp. 102–103.

2. Philip Kotler, handwritten notes prepared for introduction to a conference on design sponsored by Northwestern University, Chicago, 1989.

3. Jeffrey Meikle, "Design in the Contemporary World," Stanford Design Forum, Pentagram Design AG, 1989, p. 21.

4. Peter Gorb, "Projects Not Cases; Teaching Design to Managers," *Management Education and Development,* vol. 18, pt. 4, 1987, pp. 299–307.

Design Management Issues:
Where Does Your Company Stand On These?

- Does your CEO give visible support to design?

- Is there a senior-level design director who reports to the CEO or an executive vice president?

- Is design considered a factor for achieving strategic goals?

- Are your company's designers chained to their drafting tables, or do they participate in product planning, market research, and strategy meetings?

- Do the designers "receive" product briefs, or do they help formulate them?

- At what point in the product creation process do designers usually begin their participation?

- Do you know of an example in which designers led an initiative that resulted in a true innovation?

- What percentage of your company's development budget goes to design?

- Does your company have a corporate identity program, that is, a coordinated program for product design, communications (both verbal and visual), and environment design?

- Would you characterize your company's designers as capable of making a strong contribution to information about social and economic trends?

- Is your design organization responding to the globalization of your company?

- Is design an influential force for quality in your company?

- Is the director of design trained and experienced as a designer? Is he or she a respected authority on a wide range of company issues?

- Would your company invest in the education of its designers in design management?

- Could you imagine a designer as president of your company? (Norio Ohga, now president of Sony, was formerly director of design!)

PART TWO

HERMAN MILLER AND DESIGN MANAGEMENT

Herman Miller and the "Providential" Partnership with Design

God gives the milk but not the pail
ENGLISH PROVERB

The lore of great U.S. corporations and their leaders is rich in the stuff of rags to riches. The familiar story line includes a person with an uncommon vision who passionately believes in something revolutionary in the business world. This person sets out to launch a vision, often in a garage (Dr. Edwin Land, Polaroid; Steven Jobs, Apple et al.), and drives an enterprise to stunning success through the combination of obsessive dedication to an idea and brilliant application of that idea to a truly innovative product or service.

The story of Herman Miller, the internationally known furniture company, follows this scenario in broad outline but contains some unique variations. The story began with D. J. De Pree, the founder of Herman Miller, who was most certainly a man with vision. But his vision was not a gimmick of sudden enlightenment. Rather it was nurtured through the twists and turns of what he described as "providential" convergences of people, geography, timing, and events. These connections, which ultimately led to the transformation of the original Star Furniture Company, makers of reproductions of traditional European designs (called "princess" furniture) in the early 1900s, to Herman Miller, Inc., a producer of furniture systems of international reknown, were part of God's plan as far as D. J. De Pree was concerned. He was convinced that doing something of service for one's fellow humans was being obedient to the biblical commandment to love one another. D. J. believed he had a moral obligation to provide products that embodied "the quality of truth." Such products would have "unity, not a lot of contradictory features" and be "simple" so they would be "understandable" and the people who used them would say, "This is just right."[1] Subsequently, the company went on to provide innovative furniture solutions to human needs in living, working, healing, and learning environments.

Such terminology is surprising in the business world, especially from the founder and driving force behind a company considered to be the essence of innovation and sophistication in its products and image. The puzzle becomes more intriguing when the combination of a deeply religious man is put together with the small, midwest town, Zeeland, Michigan, which was home to D. J. De Pree. Zeeland, still an almost homogeneous, unchanged religious community of Dutch Reformed people (at last count a church on nearly every corner and no movie theater) is hardly the expected seed bed environment for a company that has built a multimillion-dollar business and breaks its own records in introducing radically new concepts in furniture and systems. Yet De Pree credited the local skilled work force and its devotion to quality excellence for much of Herman Miller's success. It might also be that the simple values of the people of a midwest town, when led by visionary people, are more conducive to the challenges of doing something new than the skeptics of a more sophisticated New York or Los Angeles culture.

Thus, the story of Herman Miller, how it grew, the "providential" connections of the right people at the right time in the right place, and the special company culture that developed out of these unique circumstances is one that intrigues everyone who has ever had any encounter with the company.

The story has been well documented in books by D. J. De Pree's sons, Hugh De Pree and Max De Pree, who took the hand-off from their father and successively ran the company from 1962 to the present time. Ralph Caplan, design critic and author, has also written a complete and fascinating documentation of the Herman Miller history in *The Design of Herman Miller*.[2] A brief recounting of the Herman Miller story, however, is essential for understanding why design was the bedrock on which Herman Miller grew in both size and stature in the international business community and how, although the design role was reinterpreted as a force for leading the company into new businesses and scales of operation, it has been retained as a key strategy.

FROM "PRINCESS" BUREAUS TO LEADING-EDGE MODERNISM

D. J. De Pree, joined by his father-in-law, Herman Miller, bought the Star Furniture Company in 1923, mostly because D. J. thought the company was suffering from sleepy management and mediocre quality in the furniture it produced. Renaming the company for his father-in-law, who actually had very little involvement, and upgrading the design and production quality, however, did not seem to D. J. to be the solution to what he saw as the real problem in the furniture industry at that time: Manufacturers were reactive stooges to the demands of furniture brokers and buyers.

In 1930 De Pree met Gilbert Rohde when Rohde introduced himself as a designer in search of a manufacturer for his startling ideas about modern furniture. De Pree was impressed with Rohde's concepts about new modes of living involving smaller houses and reductions in household help and about new attitudes about style.

The honest simplicity of modern furniture appealed to De Pree's moral code. Since bric-a-brac ornamentation often covered up shoddy workmanship, the clean lines of modern furniture demanded excellence in craftsmanship. The flexibility of modular furniture components also seemed to be a more humane and practical investment for modern families. Rohde found in D. J. De Pree not only a willing manufacturer but a convert to the philosophy of modern furniture as a way of life. Their collaboration set De Pree and Herman Miller on a course of risk taking on the basis of commitment to an untested design concept.

Throughout the 1930s D. J. De Pree and Gilbert Rohde taught each other about the concepts of design and the nitty gritty of selling. Because modern furniture was still so new in concept and appearance, it was difficult to sell. Always unhappy with the traditional percentage broker arrangement, De Pree concluded that only trained salespeople could sell the Rohde furniture. And only the company's own salespeople *would* sell it. For a time Herman Miller had its own sales staff servicing Rohde display rooms in several leading department stores, a precursor to establishing its own showrooms. Although showrooms are the norm today in the furniture industry, they were a sales innovation in the 1930s. Support of design innovation with fresh, new sales approaches set a course for an imaginative partnership between design and marketing.

World War II and the untimely death of Rohde in 1944 nearly short-circuited Herman Miller's foray into a design commitment to contemporary furniture. In his search for a replacement for Rohde, the writings of George Nelson, who was editor of *Architectural Forum,* caught De Pree's attention. Although Nelson had never designed any furniture, De Pree liked what he read in Nelson's articles about his ideas for new directions in design.

PIONEERING A CORPORATE IDENTITY PROGRAM

It was another "providential" meeting of two people who were right for each other at the right time. George Nelson became director of design for Herman Miller. He not only had the opportunity to apply his daring ideas about furniture design, he also became the Herman Miller mentor for design. He directed the design of all the company publications, consulted on marketing strategies, and, in general, exerted a strong influence on the design of the company. Nelson and Herman Miller together were early practitioners of what is now known as corporate identity.

As design director, Nelson introduced other designers to D. J. De Pree, most notably Charles Eames. Eames had attracted a certain amount of attention with his experimentation with bonding and shaping plywood into new forms. Eames was not only a designer of furniture but an inventor of the tools and machinery required to manipulate the new materials into new seating forms. Eames needed to find a manufacturer who could master the new fabrication techniques for materials such as poly resins, and achieve a scale of production that would make his chairs accessible to a broad market. These challenges were of the sort that appealed to D. J. De Pree.

The bold, innovative furniture designs by Nelson and Eames continued to demand unorthodox selling strategies to suit the market of the early 1950s. De Pree and his savvy sales manager, Jimmy Eppinger, together with George Nelson determined that the individual customer would be too timid to buy the visually radical designs. Their market acceptance had to be through architects, who would more readily understand and embrace the concepts of these designs and persuade clients to accept them. An equally well trained sales force was necessary to meet at a peer level with architects. It became a policy during this early introductory period of Herman Miller contemporary furniture to hire architects as salespeople. I was one of those.

LINKING DESIGN AND MARKETING

Educated as an architect, but with a strong interest in interior architecture, I was fascinated as a student by the work of Eames and Nelson and set as my personal goal to somehow become associated with Herman Miller. Being a salesman was not what I had in mind, but since the company was Herman Miller, this was not a run-of-the-mill sales job. Along with other architects, I joined Herman Miller in 1953 and began educating architects in the northeastern part of the United States to Herman Miller furniture as a new way of thinking about interior planning. The sales and marketing experience of those years was an invaluable training and exposure to business that has been a fortuitous circumstance of my own professional career.

By 1960 Herman Miller had grown from $1.7 million in annual sales in 1950 to $8.4 million. Although the residential market was the original focus of Herman Miller, it became clear during the 1950s that the designs of Nelson and Eames were highly adaptable to office and institutional settings. The production capability of the Eames chairs, for example, was appropriate for the scale of institutional use. And certainly the design of the chairs was as elegant a solution massed by the hundreds in auditoriums as it was by itself in a home. My work with the State of New York university system and as liaison to the Eames office to develop a variety of seating solutions for the burgeoning educational market led Herman Miller into uncharted waters for which a new method of marketing for mass market acceptance was prescribed.

The concept of a process that totally integrated design and marketing was launched in 1960 under the aegis of a new division, the Special Products Division, which I headed. The mission of this new division was to identify product development and marketing opportunities in the educational and institutional markets that were outside the normal conduct of Herman Miller business. My responsibilities included market research, product design and development, manufacturing coordination, marketing, sales, service, and installation. The Special Products Division had its own sales force for developing architect and educational institution acceptance of Herman Miller products for mass use.

DESIGN LEADS THE COMPANY TO NEW BUSINESSES

Eames's educational seating led Herman Miller into the systems business. The systems approach was basic to Charles Eames's design philosophy of refining a concept to satisfy a new user need. For example, a molded fiberglass shell, which was originally designed for residential use, and even in this form took on new identities on different bases and with upholstered pads, was adapted to institutional use with tandem bases, tilt/swivel mechanisms, and special use elements such as writing tabs. The systems concept was a key factor in Herman Miller's ability to move from residential to institutional product design and to tap large-growth markets.

It is also worth noting that Charles Eames denounced innovation as a strategic corporate goal. He insisted that quality was the essential goal to strive for. Inherent in his definition of quality was the layering of incremental refinements and improvements on a basic, good concept. Charles Eames was a master of this approach; the Japanese have proved its validity by capturing world markets in product area after product area, not by innovation, but by incremental design and technology refinements.

The Eames systems approach at that time took a new direction in a comprehensive furniture and storage system for student dormitory rooms. I was heavily involved in intensive market research for this system, but its careful design and market launch fell victim to the upheaval that swept college campuses across the United States in the mid-1960s. The story of how all the right planning and right product can be betrayed by social or political events is documented in the case study for this project.

Charles Eames and his staff designers were key to our ability to respond to the dynamic growth in the education market in the 1950s. Our approach to problem solving for specific client needs, which usually led to the development of products for wide market application, opened up opportunities beyond the education institution market.

Notable among these was the O'Hare Airport seating project in 1962. My meeting with the architects to discuss their need for a specially designed telephone booth seat led to the design of Eames Tandem Seating for O'Hare Airport public spaces and airline lounges. Today, 30 years later, the original seating is still doing service and looking good at Chicago's O'Hare Airport. It is also to be found in airports all over the world. This product, which set a quality standard for design and serviceability for airport seating, began its life as a niche product (designed expressly for O'Hare) that grew to a mass application standard. This pattern was continued in projects with Reynolds Metals for executive seating (Eames Soft Pad Chairs), John Deere, and the Ford Foundation (Eames Executive Seating).

The 1960s also marked Herman Miller's serious incursion into the office furniture market. Although as far back as 1942 the company had produced executive desks and credenzas during the Rohde era and carried forward by Nelson for the executive office market, our presence in this market segment took a new direction when our attention focused on office systems.

My own role at Herman Miller had evolved from that of "special products" design management to director of product planning design and development. The ambiguity of the "product planning" title arose from the delicate transition of the design director role of George Nelson to the internal management of design by Herman Miller. By 1967 I was named vice president of design and

Figure 4-1. The Herman Miller design team photographed in 1975 at the Walker Museum in Minneapolis with D. J. De Pree. Seated from left: Alexander Girard, George Nelson, Ray Eames. Standing from left: Robert Propst, Robert Blaich, D. J. De Pree, Charles Eames. (*Melissa Brown, photographer*)

development, and until my departure from Herman Miller in 1979 my design management responsibilities spanned the range of product design, development, facilities design, and corporate communications activities. (Figure 4-1 shows the Herman Miller design team in 1975.)

As vice president for product planning and development, my first project outside the Eames office was the management of the Nelson office's project to expand the design of their Comprehensive Storage System (CSS), consisting of shelves, storage cases, and desks which were designed to be mounted on a modular pole system. In a major project for the Federal Reserve Bank of New York, we negotiated a joint venture with Hauserman Partitions Company to develop a system of walls and wall-mounted furniture. Building on this project, we developed a freestanding panel system to replace the traditional "bull pen" office. Although the product was too expensive and too complex, it gave us both entry into the office market and experience with the concept of open land-scape office systems. CSS was the precursor of Herman Miller's Action Office, which revolutionized office design with its open office system of panels and panel-mounted work surfaces and storage components and gave birth to a multimillion-dollar industry.

DESIGN AND THE MULTIMILLION-DOLLAR OFFICE BUSINESS

The story of Action Office has several beginnings. But the source of this totally new vision of how an office ought to function and how support systems of furniture and accessories can enable people to work more efficiently and comfortably was Robert Propst.

In another fortuitous encounter, D. J. and Hugh De Pree (who had become CEO in 1962) met Robert Propst, inventor and sculptor. Propst seemed to the De Prees to be the answer to their growing conviction that Herman Miller needed to significantly diversify beyond its successful chair business. It was also becoming clear that the company needed to expand its talent resources beyond Eames and Nelson, whose interests were broadening beyond Herman Miller and furniture design.

Propst had inventions on his workbench for everything from a timber harvester to a revolutionary roofing system. Propst was *not* a furniture designer, although some of his inventions included furniture hardware mechanisms. Herman Miller established a Research Division with Propst as its head. His charter was to run with a batch of some 32 inventions, leading Herman Miller far afield from furniture. Such diversification dreams were the stuff of the 1960s for corporations in the United States and Europe. With all the wisdom of hindsight, it was Herman Miller's good fortune that Propst's interests, as far ranging as they were, began to center on furniture-related concepts, thus sparing Herman Miller the costly mistake of diversifying beyond what it had done so well.

Propst's consuming interest became focused on office environments. His research on the problems of space, comfort, health, efficiency, and human interaction in the office was aided and abetted by his frustration in his own work environment with existing office "furniture," including that of Herman Miller.

When Propst was setting up his Herman Miller research offices in Ann Arbor, Michigan (in a garage, of course), he ordered the critically acclaimed Nelson Comprehensive Storage System. He encountered much difficulty in installing the system and, worse, found that it didn't solve basic problems of paper storage and responsiveness to everyday work habits.

After exhaustive research into the office as a work environment, Propst's concepts and the Nelson office's design interpretation of these ideas was introduced as Action Office (AO). My role had evolved to that of full responsibility for all design and development activities so that I was now also acting as the coordinator for the Nelson office work with Herman Miller as well as with the Eames office projects.

The critical reception of Action Office was a resounding success primarily because it was such a startling innovation in the office furniture industry. But the design execution of Action Office by the Nelson office fell far short of Propst's concepts because it consisted basically of individual pieces of furniture rather than the fully coherent system of space dividers, work surfaces, and storage components that Propst had envisioned.

Now that the concept had been publicly introduced, Hugh De Pree worried that others would develop the concept and tap the burgeoning office construction potential. The problems Herman Miller had to overcome and the marshaling of effort and resources that was required to develop and introduce the new version of Action Office, which was simply called Action Office 2 (AO2), is described in the AO2 case study in Chapter 5. The successful outcome is well known, but what is worth emphasizing in studying projects such as AO2 is that the decision to go forward absolutely signified a critical juncture for the company. The decision was a huge risk in terms of the resources required, and it also placed the company's reputation on the line. But the alternative to the decision to proceed was to lose leadership in an idea that was clearly ready to be developed.

The magnitude of the risk was keenly understood by Hugh De Pree when he gave the "go" signal to the four-person AO2 task force, of which I was the member responsible for design and development. I recall that he told us we must do "everything short of selling the company" to succeed. Our mission was clear, and the organizational support was total.

The AO2 project also marked another important benchmark for Herman Miller. Tension had festered between Propst's Research Division and the Nelson office during the development of the first-generation AO. Neither group had proved able to merge concept, problem-solving, and design execution into an acceptable resolution. By the time Hugh De Pree's directive to proceed with AO2 was given in 1967, the primary responsibility for design had been withdrawn from both the Nelson and Propst offices. Design responsibility was under my direction, with the Research Division acting as consultants to the project. Hugh De Pree notes in his book, *Business As Unusual,* that the decision to vest the primary responsibility for design with Herman Miller "...would be a huge step away from our historic position regarding designers. The designer, we had always insisted, studied the needs, solved the problem. Our responsibility was to bring the product to the market."[3]

AO2 and the growth explosion it generated for Herman Miller in the next decade provides a classic example of how a clear mission; total management support, starting with the president; and symmetry between design and development (engineering), manufacturing, costing, and marketing in their teamwork are the essential requisites to a successful product launch.

AT ISSUE: CONSULTANTS OR IN-HOUSE DESIGN STAFF

In the aftermath of the AO2 introduction in 1968, the management of design, which had been fundamentally reformulated to the requirements of launching AO2, evolved to adjust to its expanded role. The internal design group, which I directed, had grown significantly in its stature and capabilities during the AO2 design and development years. It seemed a matter of course that the group could play a role beyond behind-the-scene design support for consultant designers.

Since both Charles Eames and George Nelson were increasingly interested and involved in design projects beyond furniture and Herman Miller, our mutual dependence was becoming a matter of history. Herman Miller had already recognized that it needed to discover new talent when it recruited Propst. The design talent search took on fresh urgency once the dust settled after the AO2 launch. That design talent search was also my responsibility.

California designers Don Chadwick and Bruce Burdick were signed on in the early 1970s as consultant designers during this period (see Figure 4-2). Chadwick interested me because he had experience with designing for rigid urethane technology (see Figure 4-3), and Herman Miller needed to continue to introduce seating solutions for the office environment. In an interesting change in our marketing push-pull impulse, AO2 created office chair and seating opportunities in contrast to the earlier opportunity openings for office furnishings generated by Eames's chairs and seating. Chadwick's association with Herman Miller was a response to this development.

Bruce Burdick's design interests promised to fill the executive office niche formerly provided by the Nelson office designs. His "Burdick Group" collection, introduced in 1980, handsomely fulfilled this expectation. Figure 4-4 shows office design from the Burdick System.

By the end of the 1960s Herman Miller was seriously working to restructure and expand its international business. The company had already developed a

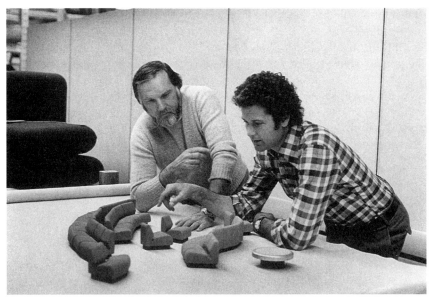

Figure 4-2. Don Chadwick and Robert Blaich discussing the model for rigid urethane modular seating.

Figure 4-3. Installation of Chadwick seating.

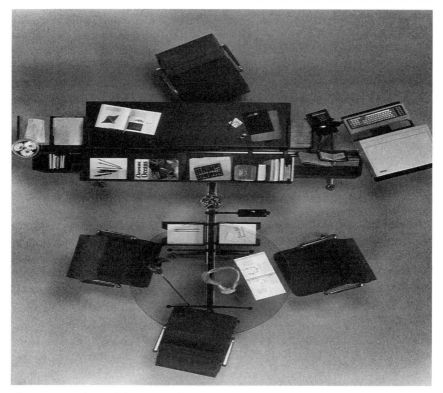

Figure 4-4. The Burdick System reflected the high-tech office environment resulting from the huge influx of electronic equipment in the 1980s. (*Courtesy of Burdick Group*)

well-established license network in Europe. Some inevitable conflicts with this arrangement arose over the degree to which our licensees were able to adapt to Herman Miller's fully concentrated efforts in the office and institutional market. Our licensees were, for the most part, much more attuned to the residential market, which by 1970 Herman Miller had almost completely abandoned in the United States.

The goal was for eventual full control by Herman Miller of our European operations. As an interim measure, I succeeded Max De Pree as managing director of Herman Miller AG, a company half-owned by Herman Miller and half-owned by Willy Fehlbaum, our former Swiss licensee. My mission in Europe was twofold: to strengthen the management of Herman Miller AG and, still continuing my responsibilities as director of design and development, to search for new design talent in Europe for Herman Miller's worldwide design program. I was also chartered to introduce AO2 in Europe.

There was no dearth of choice of new design talent. By the end of my European tour of duty I had sought out and elicited interest in working with Herman Miller from an illustrious roster of designers. The group included well-known designers such as Fritz Haller, Poul Kjaerholm, Vernor Panton, Olivier

Mourque, Hans Hollein, Pierre Paulin, and Amilio Ambasz. However, only designs from Fritz Haller, Vernor Panton, and Poul Kjaerholm were developed and produced. By the mid-1970s Action Office had so consumed Herman Miller with its success demands that niche products were unable to gain the attention and commitment of the marketing management.

Action Office had provided the springboard for a new system researched and conceptualized by Propst called "Coherent Structures" (Co/Struc). Co/Struc, like Action Office, germinated out of Propst's frustration with inadequate equipment to respond to needs. As Propst lay in a hospital bed recovering from an operation, he observed the inefficiencies and threat to health of the equipment, supplies, and furnishings used in hospitals. From that experience came a coherent system of materials-handling equipment that offered a completely new approach to cost controls, ease of use, and sanitation management in hospitals. Co/Struc also put Herman Miller into a new business sector: health care.

The concepts of Co/Struc and Action Office were then merged and designed to produce a system for factory floor work situations. This system was called "Action Factory." The focus on office and institutional systems has continued to dominate the company's product approach to the present time.

DESIGN MANAGED BY MARKETERS

By the mid-1970s the structure of the company had also changed to reflect its diversification in office and institutional, health, and factory systems. The organization shifted to divisionalization, with the product managers of each division demanding their own design teams. The strong design management direction that had guided Herman Miller, first by George Nelson, then by Hugh De Pree, and finally by myself passed into the hands of the marketers.

My role by 1976 was partially defined by my title, director of corporate design and communications. On one hand it expanded the design management responsibility to include all external and internal communications, exhibitions, and facilities design. On the other hand, with each division manager controlling design and development activities, there was no meaningful overall direction of product design. Consultant designers no longer had a "champion" to evaluate, give advice about, and steer their ideas through the design/development process. The strong design management connection between designers and the internal organization was fundamentally diminished.

For a time, the consequences of this situation appeared to be minimal in their impact. In fact, the tremendous success of Action Office spilled over to a new office system called "Ethospace Interiors," which was a softer, more humane version of the panel, component, and accessory approach to office systems. This system and the resoundingly successful ergonomic office chairs, the Equa and Ergon Chairs, led Herman Miller into the 1980s with escalating sales volume and enviable profits.

But at the beginning of the 1990s, it appeared that no furniture manufacturer, including Herman Miller, was coming forth with the kind of design leadership for setting new benchmarks for the industry that Eames seating systems, Action Office, and Ethospace Interiors had. The furniture industry, like the building industry, seemed exhausted by the boom of the last two decades.

In an industry that will have to work very much harder to sell its products to companies and institutions whose capital investment budgets are under intense constraints, the me-too products of recent years seem to be a sign that the industry is waiting for a Herman Miller–like breakthrough to new ideas and new energy.

REFERENCES

1. D. J. De Pree, tapes of an oral history of Herman Miller.
2. Ralph Caplan, *The Design of Herman Miller,* Watson Guptil, N.Y., 1976.
3. Hugh De Pree, *Business As Unusual: The People and Principles at Herman Miller,* Herman Miller, Zeeland, Michigan, 1986, p. 89.

CHAPTER FIVE

Herman Miller Case Studies and Design Management Issues

CASE STUDY:
EAMES CONTRACT STORAGE (ECS)

The special problems of the postwar boom in college education and the accompanying demand for equipment, furnishings, and buildings were of keen interest to Charles Eames. All aspects of education were, in fact, an enduring interest, leading to his later involvement in films and exhibitions as learning techniques. In his final years, Eames developed a great fascination for the possibilities of linking technology and learning.

In the early 1960s, Eames was tinkering with a system of components for college dormitory rooms that would supply a maximum amount of storage, living, and work space in a space- and cost-efficient way. The heart of his concept was a series of knockdown components that could be easily assembled and reassembled in various configurations. The system was intended as a replacement for the static and usually low-quality millwork normally installed in dormitory rooms.

As head of the newly formed Special Products Division organized to market systems such as this one, which was predictably called Eames Contract Storage (ECS), it was my task to put the design concept together with potential users. I crisscrossed the country talking to architects for colleges and universities, university specifiers, and facilities managers to discuss the problems of dormitory design and maintenance, and, in particular, the kind of furnishings that would withstand student wear and tear yet provide an amenable living environment. The problems I communicated to Eames as a result of my discussions with university administrators were ingeniously addressed in the final system design.

The primary consideration—space efficiency, and therefore cost advantages in the expensive construction costs of dormitory buildings—was the philosophic impetus for the system concept. The flexible system with its standardized components, which could be attached or detached without damage to the building structure, enabled the room dimensions to be smaller, yet achieve a feeling of

Figure 5-1. Eames Contract Storage System was an elegant solution to tough economic and use requirements of college dormitory furnishings. (*Furniture designed by Charles and Ray Eames*)

spaciousness that traditional loose furniture and traditional built-in millwork fail to do (see Figure 5-1).

The multiple demands on the normal dormitory room to accommodate sleeping, studying, storage, and leisure activities generally result in a chaotic environment. ECS organized these various activities by means of vertical panel dividers enclosing components for sleeping (a pull-down bed that could be stored out of the way during the day, and, incidentally, put the typical unmade bed out of sight), studying, and storage units.

ECS was a wall-hung system that left ample space between floor and ceiling for accessible floor cleaning and provided ventilation through the storage units to combat the effects of wet towels, sweat suits, and dirty socks. The shelves and drawers in the closets were of vinyl-coated wire, allowing the dirt and detritus of student habits to filter down through the open wire shelves to reach the floor for the occasional cleanup to put things right. Amenities such as vanity mirror, towel rod, laundry basket in the storage closet, built-in lighting, file and pencil drawers, and adjustable shelves for the study unit went well beyond those provided by standard millwork built-ins.

The Eames concern for quality was manifest in the materials and their usage. Drawers slid smoothly over vinyl-coated tracks; the divider panels were coated with a phenolic skin for durability; the bed was operated by a sophisticated counterbalanced spring assembly that was activated by a foot pedal; the continuous extruded aluminum hinge connecting doors to panels supported a weight of 500 pounds—far more than normal usage would require.

During the design process, we simultaneously considered how we would market the system. Selling the concept was especially difficult for two reasons: First, it required communicating to a multilayered tier of university decision makers, and second, the idea of a prefabricated system was so new that school purchasing agents, in particular, were nervous because they had nothing to compare it to.

My financial resources for marketing were nearly nonexistent, so the key communication problem was how to explain a new system, which could not, for logistical reasons, physically be shown to them. I asked Eames to produce a film to explain the complex subject and solution in a simple way. I could then show such a film to the variety of audiences I needed to reach.

For a modest and unprecedented $10,000 Eames produced a masterful film that combined a bit of humor about student living habits with a clever depiction of the concept of component utility, flexibility, and economy.

We designed a simple brochure as a handout to accompany the film. As part of my presentation, I passed around a door handle for the system, which in its sculptural beauty and high-quality casting was a self-proclaimed message of quality. The Eames office also built an exquisite scale model with fully working parts to show to audiences.

Although the initial cost of the installed system was 50 percent higher per room than the normal cost of millwork and individual pieces of furniture, the estimated savings over the long term in durability, part replacement, and maintenance costs brought the system into a competitive price range. Further savings could be realized in the design of the dormitory rooms in new buildings if the architect could work to the specifications of the system. It was essential, therefore, to secure early agreement from everyone concerned to specify ECS in order to achieve optimum cost benefits. Installations for new dormitories in which ECS was "designed in" yielded a space saving of 40 square feet per room, allowing for as much as 46 percent more student accommodation in comparison to the traditional space/accommodation ratio.

A pilot installation project was installed in a low-security home for delinquent girls in Detroit. There was keen interest among architects and university officials who came to see the installation, given the especially hard-use conditions of this particular environment. The system was launched with the assistance of a small specialized sales force under my direction, resulting in a number of installations across the country.

However, good as the product was, it fell victim to an entirely unpredicted social change: the student upheaval of the 1960s. None of my careful research with university officials, the Education Facilities Laboratory, architects, or Dodge Reports on the projected growth of dormitory construction anticipated the student revolts that swept college campuses. Just one of the impacts from that tumultuous time was the contempt of students for the regimentation of dormitory living. Students left campus dormitories in droves to live independently in nonuniversity apartments. And ECS was suddenly a product without users. The bottom had simply dropped out of the dormitory market.

But nothing as good as that system design can disappear without leaving some benefits behind. The things we learned from designing, producing, and marketing ECS have helped pave the way for meeting later Action Office challenges. Panel technology, production, and installation lessons from ECS were applied to Action Office. And we learned that when you are working with a complex set of users you have to develop a seamless strategy for the design and marketing of the system, bringing fresh and creative methods of communicating with your potential users about totally new concepts and products.

ECS AND
DESIGN MANAGEMENT ISSUES

Herman Miller's foray into the institutional market with individual pieces of furniture for college and university lobbies, cafeterias, libraries, and other public areas and the subsequent move into the large-scale seating systems of Eames Educational Seating positioned the company strongly in the educational market, which was spending large amounts of money in the 1950s and 1960s for capital investments to meet the demand of a burgeoning student population.

The inadequate furnishing solutions for dormitory rooms was an obvious signal for my attention and became an appealing problem challenge to Charles Eames. Tackling that issue was a valid extension of the company's focus on the education market. *The strong design initiative and management of ECS was a contribution to the strategic goals of the company,* since by the mid-1960s almost one-third of Herman Miller's annual revenue was being generated by the education market. That the market potential would dramatically change was a sociopolitical wild card.

The *scope of design work* in this project, as in nearly all Herman Miller product creation, was broad. Design work included market and design research; materials and components sourcing; engineering and production input; marketing planning and implementation; sales management; installation; and quality control monitoring. The design management role, in short, was one of complete and complex coordination of the project.

Several of these tasks deserve some further explanation. My extensive involvement in the materials and supplier sourcing and engineering and production development activities was a result of the fact that Herman Miller at that time did not have an engineering staff. All the engineering design work was done by the consultant designers in conjunction with the Herman Miller Technical Center and production engineers. My role was that of liaison between the three groups. The Technical Center, which was the first of its kind in the furniture industry, was the center of competence for researching and testing new materials and prototypes for a variety of durability and quality characteristics. This system of task assignment in which I acted as coordinator worked well, in my opinion, because it was design-driven. The Eames products were especially demanding in their technical specifications, because, quite simply, Eames was devoted to the application of new technologies for problem solving. Not surprisingly, the product designers working in his office such as Don Albinson, Dick Donges, Bob Staples, Dale Bauer, and Gordon Ashby were all "expert tinkerers." They understood mechanics and were fascinated by new materials and technical processes. They could sit down with suppliers and design the tooling or scout out the coating processes they needed. They knew how things worked, and they knew how to use new materials and techniques to advantage.

Though many Herman Miller products were based on technical innovation, the company itself at that time was not vertically organized for the production of high-tech products. The firm was basically a manufacturer of upholstered and wood products and an assembler of metal parts sourced by outside suppliers. The coordination among the purchasing department, suppliers, our Technical Center, and production engineers was a design management task inherent in all product creation activities during the period of my involvement from the 1950s to the end of the 1970s.

The entire design-to-market process was integrated in my small Special Products Division. My objectives were to identify emerging market opportunities, design and develop products and systems to meet these new needs, and devise appropriate marketing and sales strategies to achieve sales volume. My mission, in the larger sense, was to put Herman Miller in the institutional and commercial markets.

The completely integrated design-to-market process, which gained its impetus from design research and which was managed from these beginnings through to the sales, installation, and service functions with a tightly controlled, design-oriented focus, is a pure example of the coherence design management can achieve. The significant difference between *design* management and *marketing* or *product* management should be clear from this case study as well as others in Part 2. Both design management and product management are committed to achieving profits for the corporation. But design management builds its program on the premise that the client or user is the main concern. The product or system design is based on identifying a user need, and the physical realization of the product is a result of a carefully nurtured, integrated process that gives guidance to the design and development, marketing sales, and service activities. Product management, however, focuses on achieving market share. Its product design conceptions are more likely to be rooted in responses to what the competitor is doing.

The concept of a completely integrated design-to-market process as the responsibility of a design manager, illustrated in this case study, supports the premise that a *fundamental design manager characteristic* is that she or he is a generalist. The design management capabilities in the ECS/Special Projects Division director role required a large basket of general skills. An instinct for a need that had not yet been clarified by those associated with the user group (education facility professionals) was important. The role required the ability to communicate the problem and requirements to the design specialist (consultant, in this case) in a language that was appropriate and acceptable. The ability to communicate to the user audience in acceptable and persuasive language was equally necessary. A general knowledge of material processes, tooling techniques, and production engineering was essential to the product development stage to facilitate the translation of the design concept to production feasibility, and, in particular, to ensure that technical decisions did not compromise the integrity of the design. And finally, the design manager needs to have a keen affinity for marketing, as this project demonstrates. The overriding concern of the design manager is that the marketing program is appropriate for the product and the user. And finally, contact with the sales and service function delivers firsthand the hard realities of the marketplace. It is the final conclusive test of whether the product concept and realization were valid.

Eames Contract Storage was on course for becoming a solid product success. That its life cycle was shortened was one of the minor fallouts from the student rebellion against the education system of the United States in the 1960s. However, the process that delivered ECS as a product was valid. Current discussions about what design management should be has numerous references in this case study about the Herman Miller Special Products Division operating function in the 1960s. The process exemplified in this case study might be worth examining as a model for small and medium-size companies. This design management case study might also serve as a model for an integrated advanced design team and could have some relevance for developing lifestyle research capabilities.

CASE STUDY:
EAMES EDUCATIONAL SEATING (EES)

The education explosion in the post–World War II years was barely coped with in terms of buildings and equipment. Temporary shelters of all kinds were finally being replaced in the 1950s with permanent facilities after a decade of "making do." One of the unmet needs was the lack of appropriate seating for classrooms, auditoriums, and specialized learning labs.

Herman Miller had entered the education market during the late 1950s during my years as regional sales manager of the Northeast. We supplied Eames Chairs for dining halls, lounges, libraries, and student dormitory rooms for the State of New York university system. But sturdy as Eames Chairs were, they were not intended for the extreme abuse students inflicted on them.

During my personal calls on university administrators and architects, I learned about research work being done by Rensselaer Polytechnic Institute and the Ford Foundation–sponsored Educational Facilities Laboratories. On behalf of Herman Miller I joined this team in an effort to identify the problems and needs of educational facilities. In particular, the study focused on seating for classrooms and auditoriums. Nothing existed in the market that provided continuous fixed seating with a writing surface let alone that met the criteria specified by our research team for durable, comfortable, and aesthetically pleasing seating that could be installed in the most economic space allotment.

Herman Miller's design solution was to adapt the famous Eames plastic shell seat to produce a family of products for inclined or step-and-riser installation,

Figure 5-2. The extension and refinement of the classic Eames shell seat put Herman Miller into the educational facilities business in a big way. (*Furniture designed by Charles and Ray Eames*)

with swivel mechanisms, tilt mechanisms, drop-hinge tablet arms, or for placement at tables. (See Figure 5-2.) The shell seats, which were reengineered to be strengthened with more fiberglass, could either be arranged on a fixed pedestal or mounted on inclined or level floors in straight or radius configurations. Charles Eames was enthusiastic about the problem definition of the project and, as always, was challenged by pushing an existing product to new limits in technology and design problem solving.

I recall that I organized a hands-on work meeting between Eames and the owner of a small tool-and-die shop in Spring Lake, Michigan. (Because of the demand for tool-and-die suppliers for the automobile industry, Michigan had a number of experts in this area.) Eames and the tool-and-die man passed a pencil back and forth to make changes in Eames's preliminary drawing, discussing design possibilities and die casting limitations to hammer out a feasible design for the bases that would carry the mounted plastic shells. Working directly with the supplier at the design concept stage was an Eames work style that has been too much neglected by product designers and developers in recent years.

Bob Staples, the Eames office designer assigned to this project, recalls that he and I were in New York to present the final die-cast drawings to Charles Eames for approval. We were on our way to the die caster after that meeting when Eames notified us he had changed his mind about the shapes and wanted to switch to sand castings. "It was back to the drawing board," comments Staples. This painstaking striving for perfection was an Eames hallmark, and it required those of us involved in projects to flow with the endless design changes.

The resulting family of educational seating systems put Herman Miller for the first time truly in the mass market arena. Thousands of seats in their many variations were sold to colleges and universities, beginning with massive installation as a result of specification standardization within the State of New York university system and spreading across the country. University and college specifiers are a close fraternity. News of a good or, conversely, a flawed product spreads via the tom-tom system. Failure is not tolerated, and word-of-mouth references are the primary sales medium.

The message the specifiers spread was that the Herman Miller seating system was cost competitive; it had added value in the hinged tablet arms, swivel mechanism, and radius configuration. Moreover, it was easy to install and maintain. Architects favored the seating because the Eames reputation for quality and design prestige flattered their buildings. The product system was so successful that Herman Miller, in effect, prototyped the market for the flood of copies that inevitably followed. By the mid-1960s the education market accounted for about 25 percent of the company's total sales volume.

EES AND
DESIGN MANAGEMENT ISSUES

The success of EES as a mass market system of products can, in retrospect, be seen as a fundamental benchmark in the history of Herman Miller and its evolution from a manufacturer of residential and executive office furniture to the second largest (after Steelcase, Inc., Grand Rapids, Michigan) producer of systems for the office and institutional market. At the time, although the goal to focus on this market was not clearly identified, the Special Products Division, which I headed, did have a mandate to put Herman Miller in the education and special contract business.

Thus, the groundwork was being laid by my small division to lead the company into new product areas and new markets. The EES program can be seen as a major contributor to *establishing strategic direction* for Herman Miller for the next three decades.

The *scope of design work* in this project was and remains today typically unorthodox in design management in that my role as design manager involved direct contact with the potential client, in this case the State of New York university system. My role also involved participation in research with EFL and Rensselaer Polytechnic Institute to study the problems of student facility seating and to develop needs criteria.

During the product creation process, I was directly engaged in finding suppliers and component producer sources and acted as facilitator among these people, the consulting designer, and the university administrative officials. Installation of the seating required direct monitoring. Since the installation procedures were designed into the product, controlling and monitoring this activity was also my responsibility.

Clearly, design was integrated into the product creation process ranging from rudimentary discussions about seating problems to feedback about on-site performance of installed EES. In fact, the project is a clearcut example of *design-led innovation:* problem identification, research, product creation, product manufacture, installation, and monitoring of feedback. The particularly unorthodox additional activity was that of salesmanship. I made the contacts with university officials and architects and persuaded them that Herman Miller could design and produce the product that met their needs.

With the strong focus on the consumer as the business theme of this decade, the direct contact between the design manager and clients during all phases of the research-to-market (and follow-up service) stream in this project points to a model that companies might do well to introduce into the product creation process.

This project is also another example of *design as a force for quality.* It was an Eames hallmark to *design quality into the product.* This is a phrase that is rather often used today in discussions about the design-to-market process. However, I have observed few real examples that surpass or even equal Charles Eames's accomplishment, in fact, insistence, on this point. The long life of his product installations attest to both performance durability and aesthetic classicism. Perhaps the inherent designed-in quality of Eames products such as EES can be attributed to his explanation that he was essentially an architect, and product design, in his opinion, has to do with structure, just as architecture does.

In the matter of installation, for example, Bob Staples designed the aluminum substructures for either the inclined, step-and-riser version, or the straight or radius row configuration so that the legs carry long parallel rods to which the shell seats are bolted. Since the only permanent attachments are the legs, the on-site installation of a complete seating system is greatly simplified because all the rest of the components are preassembled at the factory. Thus installation equipment and worker-hour requirements are at a minimum, reducing the total system costs.

Other rigorous specifications related to fire-proof requirements for the shell seats, quick-swing compliance for the arm tabs, maneuverability specifications between rows and tab arms, and, of course, material strength to resist heavy abuse are all designed into the system. At the same time, the aesthetic character of the seating has an ageless simplicity of form.

Designed-in quality also allowed variations to the basic system to be developed for specific school requirements, which my in-house design team designed for numerous later projects.

CASE STUDY:
EAMES TANDEM SEATING

This design project illustrates how experience in designing and developing a basic component can be a springboard for the leap into a completely new market. The case study also demonstrates how a design manager can identify and act upon the possibilities for design-led product innovation that can lead to a new business opportunity.

Anyone who travels by air anywhere in the world is familiar with Eames Tandem Seating. It is installed in airports of all sizes all over the world, and, because it was designed for durability (the original O'Hare tandem seating bases, installed in 1962, are still supporting weary travelers 30 years later), the next generation of travelers are likely to be just as familiar with this ubiquitous but elegant seating.

The project started when Harvey Stubsjoen, project architect for C. F. Murphy Associates, which was given the commission to design O'Hare Airport, contacted me to talk about an idea he had for specially designed telephone booth seating. I directed the discussions to the subject of the kind of seating that would be specified for the general public areas. Stubsjoen admitted that this was a problem; nothing appropriate existed. The brief I asked him to write was formidable in its criteria: The seating should be compatible with the International Style architecture of the O'Hare terminal buildings; durable; easily replaceable; require minimal maintenance; and cost competitive (although since no such airport seating existed, there was nothing with which to compare price). The architects also insisted on comfort, which they felt was notoriously absent in existing airport seating. The greatest challenge in the brief, however, was the time frame. There was a scant year to design, tool, produce, and install the seating. We estimated tooling time alone would take six to eight months.

My strategy was to pique Charles Eames's interest in this project, believing that it would be possible to build on our experience with the aluminum castings of the Eames Aluminum Group. As I had hoped, Eames was enthusiastic about the problem-solving aspects of the project. By the time Stubsjoen visited Eames in his Venice, California, office to discuss the brief, Eames already had mock-ups to show Stubsjoen. The Eames design vocabulary had strong appeal to the architects. The innovation in the design consisted of a "sandwich" construction of foam heat-sealed between two sheets of vinyl to form interchangeable seat and back components. These were then tension-mounted between the interlocking aluminum frame of the seat, with a single screw beneath each armrest (easily assembled and taken apart for replacement of pads) holding the whole seat in place. Mounted on a continuous steel beam and cast aluminum pedestal base, the seats could be attached in any number desired (see Figure 5-3).

The three-way collaboration between the architects, the producer (Herman Miller), and the consultant designer (Charles Eames) demanded intense design management and liaison work. "The role of the manufacturer in such an endeavor

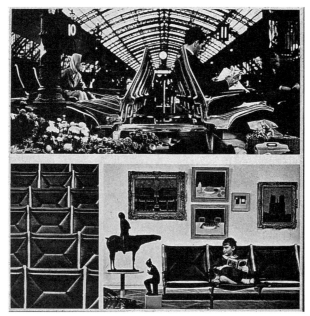

Figure 5-3. Herman Miller created a new market with its Tandem Seating design for airports. (*Furniture designed by Charles and Ray Eames*)

is interesting," said Charles Eames. "In the early stages of development Herman Miller kept a flow of information going between the architects and our office."[1]

In the later stages of the project other players joined the roster of participants to increase the complexity of the design management role: the City of Chicago, which was the ultimate client, our third-party suppliers for the aluminum castings, and the airlines, which would be requiring departure lounge seating.

The political element became particularly dicey when, on submission of bids for the project, another furniture manufacturer appeared out of nowhere with a model prototype that was a knock-off of Herman Miller's submitted design. It was apparent that our prototype model, which had been submitted to the City of Chicago purchasing office well before bid deadline, had made its debut in the model shop of a competitor. The heated meeting at City Hall during which models and bids were submitted will live forever in my memory. Well-briefed by the Herman Miller patent attorney, my strategy was to weigh in with solid patent credentials, which could be sustained should a legal showdown ensue. It also implied that the competitive model, employing these same patented heat seals, castings, and connector elements had clearly not been the result of months of design and development work by our competitor, but, in fact, had been copied from our "borrowed" prototype model.

The matter was serious, not just because Herman Miller could be in jeopardy of losing the O'Hare project. We had taken a tremendous risk in high investment costs to develop the tandem seating and in tooling up for production. The final decision to proceed with design and development was made by Hugh De Pree, then president of Herman Miller. The marketing people didn't support the project, failing to see any opportunity beyond the O'Hare Airport for the seating. But Hugh De Pree, in typical fashion, believed that if the product was well designed, it would create a market. In a *Progressive Architecture* article written after the O'Hare installation, Hugh De Pree said, "Herman Miller did not analyze the market for public seating before deciding to produce this new seating group. To be sure, we were interested in market response, but the real impetus came from a desire to see the new design become a reality. We are depending on the validity of the design and on the quality of its manufacture to create a demand for Tandem Seating."[2]

Thus, having met all the criteria with a design that was a visual and structural tour de force, it was disheartening to face the threat of losing out to a competitor who could shave its costs because we had done all the design and development work for them. In addition to highly suspected bureaucratic foul play, Mayor Daley knew an incipient lawsuit when he saw one and cast the crucial decision in favor of Herman Miller.

The seating was installed by Herman Miller when promised and was within the budget specifications. The Eero Saarinen architecture office was soon in contact with Herman Miller to investigate the possibility for installation of Tandem Seating at Dulles Airport, which was still on the drawing boards. The O'Hare installation of Tandem Seating was followed by one at Dulles Airport, and over the years by countless airports all over the world. The seating was also found to be appropriate for lobbies in office buildings and museums (see Figure 5-4).

In the decade following the introduction of Tandem Seating at O'Hare Airport, Herman Miller had captured 90 percent of the airport seating market during the period of active airport construction.

Tandem Seating has remained basically unchanged in its design. It turns up occasionally in a different color of vinyl for the seating (Charles Eames considered black to be the only suitable seating skin), and the ease of replacing worn or damaged seats while maintaining the nearly indestructible frame has proven itself in the 30 years since the product was first installed at O'Hare.

TANDEM SEATING AND DESIGN MANAGEMENT ISSUES

Because I had direct access to the president of Herman Miller, I was able to win his necessary support for what was a high-risk investment of resources. The *status of design* at Herman Miller and the direct relationship between design manager and president were the crucial points in the decision to take the risk, especially in view of the nonsupport from marketing.

The *scope of design work* in this project involved liaison work between the client, consulting designer, suppliers, toolmakers, and Herman Miller's engineering group. Since the time frame for the project was extremely short, this liaison role was critical to the project's success.

Figure 5-4. Installation of Eames Tandem Seating at Dulles International Airport. (*Furniture designed by Charles and Ray Eames*)

The project also points to the "many-hat" *role of the design manager.* Selling, which required different nuances in approach to different players in the project, was the starting point from which the project grew. First, it was necessary to appeal to the architects' interests in solving their problem. Next, came the more sensitive task of approaching Charles Eames in a way that would arouse his interest in the problem. This was always a delicate matter, because Eames was less interested in Herman Miller's strategic and market needs than in solving a specific client problem. In this case, the client problem was both clear and interesting to Eames. In the face of high risks and an unknown market demand (although we certainly knew that a high level of airport construction activity was in the wind), the project had to be sold to the president of the company on the merits of the product itself and on a large-scale, highly visible prototype installation.

The political aspects of the project necessitated hours of visits to offices of city bureaucrats, who were unimpressed with the fine points of design. Cost, maintenance, durability, and on-time delivery were the things that mattered. Cronyism to favorite, entrenched suppliers also mattered, as it turned out. The design manager, as was demonstrated rather dramatically in this project, has to be prepared to roll with punches of all kinds.

The O'Hare Tandem Seating project was clearly a *design-led innovation* for Herman Miller, taking the company into the leadership position for the airport seating market and delivering years of profitable return on investment. The opportunity was identified, acted upon, and managed through a complex web of interaction by the design manager.

Design as a force for quality was fundamental to the philosophy of Charles Eames. Although he eschewed innovation for its own sake, his obsession with building on previous design elements, technical accomplishments, and form expressions to achieve a new level of refinement very often, in fact, achieved a design innovation. Eames preferred to define these incremental improvements as quests for quality.

Building on the technical achievements of his previously designed aluminum seating group was for Charles Eames where the gravity of interest pulled him; solving the airport seating problem gave him a great reason to pursue the extension of this technical and visual direction. In the end, Eames did achieve one of the clearest examples of product innovation, whether he would agree to calling Tandem Seating innovative or not. He was certainly satisfied that he had designed a product system that demanded quality in its manufacture and produced a quality experience for the users, who in this case were the clients who must maintain the seating and the travelers who find comfort during the wearying stresses of air journeys. The design management role as coordinator of the project was crucial to its success in meeting the time requirement and satisfying the demands of a complex set of customers.

CASE STUDY:
ACTION OFFICE 2 (AO2)

The measured and leisurely pace of researching and designing a revolutionary new systems approach for offices was abruptly shoved into high gear when Herman Miller president, Hugh De Pree, attended a conference on open office landscape planning and was shocked to learn that competitors were taking Herman Miller's ideas and planning to run with them.

Herman Miller had introduced in 1964, to the acclaim of the office furniture industry and the design media, a system of office furniture components called Action Office. This market launch was the result of four years of intensive research. Long hours were spent by Robert Propst, the company's research division director, and his team in studying information genesis, flow, and control; the psychological effects of space; behavioral aspects of workers in typical work environments; implications of health with regard to work habits and spaces; productivity results in relationship to variations in office environments

Figure 5-5. Action Office was based on extensive multidisciplinary research into how people function in the office environment.

(see Figure 5-5). Anthropologists, health experts, sociologists, and psychologists were consulted. The research of numerous corporations on slices of the problems of worker performance was studied. Some companies, such as GE, were interested in fatigue factors for radar monitor technicians. Other companies studied the dynamics of paper handling or office lighting and physical reactions. Many companies seemed to know that problems abounded in the office environment and studied some of their implications. But nobody had done anything of any significance to solve the problems.

Propst was determined to be the exception. His mission was to design a system of work stations and support elements that would address the multitude of problems aswarm in the office. Principally, these included the need for flexibility as business groups or tasks change; the proliferation of information and the problem of how to store and retrieve paper; the rigid, closed environment of traditional offices that discourage meaningful communication; health and social inhibitions to productivity; costly investments to change static office spaces.

However Propst, too, became ensnared in the researcher's habit of not knowing how and when to move out of the research stage to the design and production stage. After a visit I made with Hugh De Pree to the research facility in Ann Arbor, Michigan, he said to me that we had to move the project out of Propst's hands and into a serious design phase. The crude mock-ups that Propst had managed to design to give some substance to his concepts were discouraging. De Pree remarked to me that they looked like something out of a high school manual training class. It was decided to give the design assignment to George Nelson's office. I was responsible as Herman Miller's director of product planning and development at that time to act as liaison between the Propst and Nelson offices—a role that became increasingly hazardous as the irritation level grew between the two offices as the design and production of the system components progressed.

The successful launch of Action Office was no doubt a measure of how badly a new approach to the office environment was needed. Action Office was poorly engineered with resulting structural weaknesses. It was expensive because the design of the parts was never compatible with mass production. And it was not properly marketed. The normal dealer distribution was inadequate to communicate the complex usage concepts to customers. Worse, in Propst's estimation, the tables, rolltop desks, and freestanding storage walls did not convey the true "system" concept he had intended (see Figure 5-6). The freestanding storage files that formed a sort of privacy delineation and demarcation between work stations did not sufficiently solve the problem of hanging the necessary shelf and file components for information handling. In short, Propst considered the

Figure 5-6. The open office landscape theory, which had been long talked about, became a reality with Action Office. Herman Miller once again designed and produced the prototype for the office furniture industry.

Nelson design only a modest step rather than the quantum leap forward that the serious issues he had researched warranted.

But Action Office was innovative enough to make a first step toward supplying products for the long-discussed open landscape theory, and Action Office established Herman Miller as a serious contender in the middle management office market. The system was also an elegant group of office furnishings with sufficient innovative design elements to capture the spirit of new ways of thinking about the office. It achieved the crucial breakthrough in presenting an "arena" office layout rather than the rigidly traditional rectilinear configuration. The stand-up rolltop desk with its beautifully articulated tambour cover and polished chrome pedestal legs and the accompanying roll-around "perch" seat not only were fresh and elegant, they also represented a serious attempt to define a new office-furnishing design vocabulary.

Herman Miller, as usual, was the prototype for the industry. But this time the lovely cake presented to the world was only half baked. Thus Hugh De Pree's swift call to arms, roused by the threat of someone else finishing the job that had been so exhaustively researched and expensively prototyped by Herman Miller, set into motion the second generation of Action Office, which was inevitably called Action Office 2 (AO2).

Propelled by the urgency of competitive preempting, Hugh De Pree mandated the launch of this next generation of Action Office in nine months' time. The task force he named to bear the responsibility for achieving this mandate consisted of the vice president of marketing, Glenn Walters, as chairman; I was head of design; Dick Ruch was the head of manufacturing; and Steven Snoey was the head of finance. We later added a marketing director, Joe Schwartz, to develop what the task force began to see as a completely revolutionary way to market the system.

The task force developed a critical time path system for task completion and met weekly to check progress against time targets. Although the soft blurring of time tends to focus on the heroic teamwork of this task force, I also recollect frequent pitched battles, not the least of which resulted from Propst's strong reluctance to consider any alternative to his concepts. I recall that one of my designers (all the design work was being executed by my small internal staff of about four designers plus a liaison designer from the Propst office) came up with an excellent solution for slide-mounting panel-hung components. The slide-grooved panel connector had a number of advantages against the Propst lock-in-place connector for hanging components, including easier installation and manufacturing simplification. However, Propst was unable to accept modification to his ideas.

Despite such turf-guarding skirmishes, the task force moved forward. The design challenges were essentially linked to the cost-price targets, which were immutable. The targets slashed the cost-price of Action Office first generation by several hundred percent. The incident of the vacuum-formed plastic pencil drawer illustrates the set-in-concrete cost targets. Previously the drawers had been manufactured from rather expensive materials resulting in high cost that could not be recovered. The controversy about this drawer boiled over when design and engineering had gotten stuck at the $2 or so manufacturing cost. The task force chairman at one of the weekly "wrangle sessions" finally banged his fist on the table and said, "One dollar. That's it." Somehow we had to do it. And we did. The battle to wring every penny of cost fat out of each component was cheered forward from then on by the "one dollar drawer" slogan.

Our design group worked closely with manufacturing. Since the success of AO2 depended on high volume sales, Herman Miller was being challenged to deal for the first time with true mass production (many of the Eames product components were made by suppliers) in its own factories. The design of the numerous components required the simplest possible manufacturing process.

My personal challenge was to minimize as much as possible the erosion of quality from the design quality of the original Action Office. However, elegant details such as the polished aluminum pedestals (now painted instead to save the cost of polishing) and real wood surfaces disappeared to conform to the "dollar pencil drawer" cost-measuring stick (see Figures 5-7 and 5-8).

Figure 5-7. Action Office 2 was a redesigned version of its predecessor. Lower cost, production efficiency, and a unique marketing program were strategic goals in the run-up to market launch.

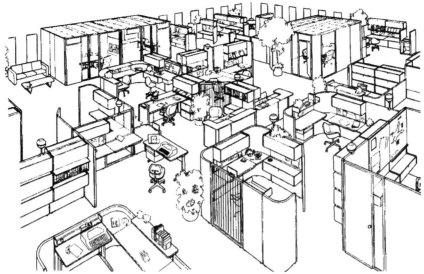

Figure 5-8. Action Office 2 led the way to the open office and panel systems boom of the 1970s. (*Drawing by Robert Propst*)

It is interesting to note that after AO2's hugely successful launch, quality and more humane design elements, such as fabric panels, wood surfaces, and storage panel options were added. But what emerged for initial introduction was a plain vanilla, no-frills product system. This was the way Propst wanted it—he had none of the aesthetic talent of Nelson or Eames—and this vision was in large part mandated by the cost constraints. As a designer, I accept that cost is nearly always a challenge to be reckoned with quality. I felt more could have been achieved to reconcile the two in a better way, and eventually we did add more design quality to the system.

There can be no argument, however, with the unqualified successful reception of AO2. The too-modest sales projections were demolished by the steep upward sales takeoff, astonishing even the most optimistic of our colleagues. The most astonished people were our manufacturing group. The avalanche of orders swamped production capacity, forcing the company to contract to local furniture factories to fabricate panels and other components and putting into motion plans for factory expansion.

No small part of the immediate success of AO2 was the marketing program, which was as revolutionary as the system itself. Our task force recognized from the lesson of the first Action Office that the normal dealer sales network was not the answer. Architects and dealers didn't have office function problems. The customer did. We needed to have direct communication with customers to explain the concepts of a totally new way of functioning in offices that AO2 offered. Customers had to understand both *why* AO2 was designed as it was and *how* they could use it to best advantage. Propst contended that Action Office was comprised of at least 50 percent information—in other words, how to use it was at least as important as the physical system itself.

The task force agreed that our New York regional sales and marketing manager, Joseph Schwartz, should be given the responsibility to develop and direct a unique marketing program. And that he did. He devised a program for inviting key potential corporate customers to come to Grand Rapids, Michigan, for the first seminars about the problems of offices and for a preview of how Herman Miller could solve these problems.

The seminars were conducted on the top floor space of a new, centrally located bank building. What went on there—the seminars—*were* truly seminars as business executives have experienced them. The seminars provided information and proposed solutions. They were not the typical sales hype. These seminars were so successful that we felt confident enough to seek more permanent facilities to continue the program as an integral part of the AO2 product system program.

We rented a vacant supermarket in a rather down-at-the-heels shopping mall in a blue-collar farm community suburb of Grand Rapids, Michigan. There was some anxiety about the off-putting environment, but I encouraged the decision to go with it because I felt the space had great potential for renovation for our use. And in addition to my design responsibilities for the product itself, I directed the facility design and renovation, transforming the supermarket into an elegant and comfortable reception area, seminar room complete with sophisticated audio visual equipment, dining room, and, not least, a complete installation demonstrating Action Office in a variety of configurations. (Interestingly, the presence of the "Education Center" motivated a brush-up of the other shopping center tenants.)

The seminars themselves were masterful. Highly professional presentations were given by outside consultants on office work psychology, productivity, information about paper handling problems, and so forth. Propst then explained his concepts based on the kind of information that had just been presented. I talked about the design of the product. Then—and only after the information seminar—the guests were shown Action Office. The magic was that by this time they understood what the Action Office was, why it looked as it did, and how it could solve their problems.

This unique marketing program was a major breakthrough. The program differed in so many ways from the usual marketing programs of most companies. It is interesting to note that the marketing was developed to satisfy the requirements of the product concept and design rather than the usual reverse situation.

AO2 catapulted Herman Miller into the office and institutional business in a big way. AO2 also created a whole new business for many other companies. As Ralph Caplan notes, the lack of visual distinction of AO2 made it much easier for competitors to copy.[3] Propst insisted on this lack of distinction, not only because he really didn't understand design finesse but also because he was determined that the design should not intrude in any way on the serious business of problem solving (which ignored the examples of Nelson and Eames, who both solved problems and did it with elegance).

The floodgates were soon opened for a huge new industry in open office and panel systems, fed by the office building boom of the 1970s. Herman Miller found itself, though it was the recognized leader, in a generational race with hosts of competitors to add design amenities and new component bells and whistles to chase the ever-ephemeral marginal distinctiveness.

AO2 AND
DESIGN MANAGEMENT ISSUES

The AO2 program was the first truly strategic product plan executed at Herman Miller. Up to this point, decisions were made about product development largely because of the opportunities presented by circumstances, often the result of interests the consultant designers wanted to pursue or building on existing products. However, the company was no stranger to creating markets for its products. In fact, in nearly every instance of successful (i.e., significant volume) products, designing and producing a product for a specific client for which a broader market subsequently developed was the modus operandi. AO2 differed in that a well-conceived strategy that involved all aspects of company operations and functions, including, for the first time, in-house design, was put into operation at the outset and executed with discipline and creativity. Design was a crucial element to *the strategic goals* of AO2 and for the larger corporate mission of focusing on the office and institutional industry.

The AO2 task force is an example of how the *integration of design* as an equal partner into the entire design-to-market process works in the best sense of the concept. Of particular note is the follow-through of the design role in the marketing of AO2, both in terms of the design of the educational center facility and participation in the seminars, giving proper *scope to design activity.*

Another noteworthy point is that the AO2 system required a significant service effort from Herman Miller in space planning and consultation with customers. This important group of designers, which I hired, trained, and managed, were interior environment specialists whose skills went beyond those of the usual interior planners. Feedback from this group was vital to the continuous generational design upgrading of the system in which we engaged.

The design responsibilities of meeting stringent budget and time targets, designing for mass production and efficiency, directing the work of the internal design group and subsequent space planning team, designing the seminar facility, and participating in the seminars themselves demonstrate how the *management of corporate resources* is both a design management opportunity and responsibility.

CASE STUDY:
CORPORATE IDENTITY AT HERMAN MILLER

From the very beginning of his association with Herman Miller, George Nelson approached his appointed role as design director from a holistic point of view. He was an early practitioner of the philosophy that a corporate identity is established and nurtured by the sum total of its activities. He taught Herman Miller that the products it designs and makes are the tangible core of the company, and these products must be supported by advertising, sales, promotional, and public relations materials that reflect the innovative character and the quality values of the products. Nelson also put his corporate identity philosophic stamp on Herman Miller by setting the standard for showroom and exhibition design and the architecture of its factories and offices.

As a result of these collectively orchestrated activities, Herman Miller was genuinely admired as much for its elegantly spare ads and crisp, contemporary showrooms as it was for its furniture. A relatively small company in the 1950s and 1960s, Herman Miller cast a large shadow in its reputation. Among architects, design professionals, furniture dealers, corporate and institutional clients, the art and design press, and even the general mass media, the quality of Herman Miller's print communications, showrooms, factories, and offices became inseparable in their minds with its furniture. This phenomenon we recognize in the 1990s as the much-vaunted but still not clearly understood corporate identity.

While Nelson's corporate identity imprimatur established the reference point that has guided the company ever since, Charles and Ray Eames and Alexander Girard also made important and lasting contributions to the substance of the design of Herman Miller's corporate identity and helped mold the company's attitude about itself. Charles and Ray Eames also designed showrooms for Herman Miller, and gave new definition to exhibition as a serious and sophisticated way to communicate information (see Figure 5-9). Their films, a number of which were produced to explain the ideas behind the Eames furniture designs, became icons among film buffs. And Charles Eames was so protective of the quality of his product designs that no ad or product brochure was ever released without meeting his demanding standards for approval.

The Eames, Nelson, and Girard offices were both amazing and stimulating laboratories for learning the lessons of the meaning and execution of all the elements that create a company's identity. The boiling pot of diverse activities— researching and designing exhibitions, designing and prototyping products, producing films, photography, and multiscreen slide shows, the designing of showrooms—all this going on in a single studio was a crucible of creativity that made a lasting impression on anyone who observed it. My own very frequent working visits to these offices left me with lifelong memories of the energy of creativity that went on in those places and with the lesson that each of the designers never considered a product, poster, exhibition design, or any other such activity in isolation from the total idea they wanted to communicate. Eames,

Figure 5-9. The design of Herman Miller showrooms was given serious attention. Eames, Girard, and Nelson all took their turn at this task, as did I as vice president of corporate design.

in particular, had a hand in everything that went on in his office. But it has to be said that the people who worked for Nelson and Eames (Girard had a very small staff) were all multitalented. Designers moved easily between product design and exhibition information research and other design tasks. It was a way of working and a way of thinking.

Alexander Girard was the third important designer for Herman Miller in the period from the 1950s to the 1980s. Like Eames and Nelson, Girard was a man of many talents. He was trained as an architect and is considered one of the premier collectors of folk art in the world. His primary contribution to Herman Miller was his fabric designs. As a colorist, Girard had few peers. His fabrics endowed the spare designs of Eames and Nelson with texture, warmth, and a grace note of human kindness. His drapery textiles and accessory objects lent a spirit of joy and whimsy to showrooms and Herman Miller customer installations, and his own design for the Herman Miller showroom in San Francisco was a delightful splash of gilt, color, and pattern.

It should be noted that Ray Eames also dispensed deft touches of grace to a variety of Herman Miller projects. Her signature heart symbol appeared with frequency, and Herman Miller has to be unique with the design of its first publicly offered stock certificate: Ray Eames designed a charming graphic screen print of a bouquet of flowers superimposed on the usual legal and financial information of such a document.

My liaison duties involved me in varying degrees in these diverse activities, so that when I assumed the duties of vice president of design and development for Herman Miller in the mid-1960s, in addition to my product design responsibilities, I also managed the entire spectrum of corporate identity activities.

The Eames, Nelson, and Girard offices continued to consult on projects in which they were interested, but other consultants were also engaged. Over a period of years I developed an in-house staff not only for product design but for certain aspects of corporate communication, such as graphic design for annual reports, stockholder communications, internal newsletters, posters, and special publications.

The years following the introduction of AO2 saw a great growth spurt. We needed to expand the factory and office facilities, and the showroom demands for larger spaces and new locations added to the facility requirements. Architect Quincy Jones was commissioned to develop a master plan for our manufacturing and office headquarter campus in Zeeland, Michigan. I was responsible for the interior architecture and planning design of the new plants and administrative offices and had the task of managing the project in consultation with Jones.

I also conducted searches for new showroom sites not only in the United States but in Europe as well, negotiating lease contracts and supervising the interior construction and design of these new, and in other cases, rehabilitated and expanded showrooms.

The Herman Miller house style program was a durable one, growing out of George Nelson's original logo design for the famous Herman Miller white "M" on a field of red-orange. He set the standard for product catalog design with excellent photography, scale diagrams, and detailed materials and parts information (see Figure 5-10). Our internal staff expanded on this model to produce a design for Herman Miller trucks and jet and to provide award-winning product literature under the direction of consultant John Massey and the work of our internal graphic designer, Stephen Frykholm.

One of the lessons Herman Miller learned from Charles Eames was that of "tak-

Figure 5-10. Herman Miller's corporate identity set a standard for reinforcing their image as an innovator.

ing your pleasures seriously." The alfresco meals served at the Eames office during midday breaks or late evening work sessions were times for the most pleasant sociability. But even the simplest of meals were, under Ray Eames's direction, presentations that should have first been photographed. The arrangement of the food, the table accessories, the bouquet of fresh flowers were the signals of a social ritual that was meant to be important enough to care about the details.

Herman Miller's annual employee picnics, although not quite the elegant presentations organized by Ray Eames, nevertheless were touched by the same caring attitude. Anyone who has ever seen Stephen Frykholm's picnic posters (see Figure 5-11), which serve as announcements to Herman Miller employees of the event, must suffer a twinge of envy at the fantasies of the good times they miss by not being a Herman Miller employee. The picnic posters, by the way, have captured design awards year after year, have become collectors' items (a valuable Herman Miller corporate image program in itself), and are in the permanent collections of art museums all over the world.

Figure 5-11. Corporate identity extends to the award-winning designs of company picnic posters.

The quality associated with "taking fun seriously" carried over to all the events hosted by Herman Miller, from showroom openings to AO2 seminars. I found it necessary to develop a staff responsible for "event management" to plan and execute such occasions with a "Ray Eames quality."

The company's attitude about itself, strongly influenced by the quality of its products, communications, and facilities, carried over into human resource management policies. Herman Miller's participatory management program, which was revolutionary in the 1960s under a scheme called the Scanlon Plan, has engendered interest and admiration worldwide. More recently, the company has looked to its linked manufacturing and environment responsibilities and attracted media attention to its waste management program and the announcement that it will no longer use endangered wood products in its furniture.

Herman Miller, clearly, is not just in the business of making furniture. If it wants to communicate the appropriate perception about its products, it must concern itself with the entire milieu surrounding the products. The only way to do it right is to do it completely. This is a concept only a handful of companies have executed with disciplined consistency over the long period required to establish and maintain a corporate identity.

CORPORATE DESIGN AND COMMUNICATIONS AND DESIGN MANAGEMENT ISSUES

Nothing will proclaim the *status of design* in a corporation more forcefully than a totally integrated corporate identity program. Herman Miller, Apple, Olivetti, IBM, Braun, Bang and Olufsen, and a scattering of other companies do not become embroiled in the issue of the importance of design to their activities. Their products, advertising, corporate facilities, promotional literature, in short, all their visual, written, and environmental activities are tangible evidence that design is embedded in the bones and muscle of their companies. It is there for everyone to see—customers, employees, stockholders, the media.

It is also obvious from the Herman Miller example that the *scope of design work* goes well beyond product design or attractive advertisements. A well-planned and coordinated cluster of product design, verbal and visual communication design, and facility design produce a synergy that acts as a powerful *force for quality* in everything a company does. The point was made earlier that discussions of quality focus primarily on engineering and production. There is a lot of hand-wringing speculation about how workers can be motivated to achieve desirable standards of quality. Leadership role models, group interaction, and remuneration incentives are certainly not to be discounted. But attitudes as part of the corporate culture are also influenced by the more subtle but pervasive examples of quality that surround employees. The cluster of corporate design and communications signposts for quality—products, communications, and the physical environment in which they work—send strong messages about the kind of standards a company sets for itself.

A stroll through Herman Miller headquarters offices or its factories makes the point with utmost clarity. The quality of the architecture, the imaginative interior layouts, designs and the creative use of designed amenities, even in such normally mundane fixtures as time reporting systems, send several levels of messages. First, it is obvious this is a company that cares about its employees. Second, the company has a tradition of quality standards that the employees should understand and accept responsibility for perpetuating; the standards are not something abstract that are being preached about but have a tangible presence that permeates the employee's work life. Third, the company takes pride in what it does and how it presents itself. And the employee, because of the pervasive influence of these *designed* elements is able to honestly share in that pride. A short conversation with any Herman Miller employee confirms this point.

A case can also be made for the *importance of corporate design and communication in contributing to the strategic goals of the company*. The success of AO2 depended, obviously, on the design of the system. But the battery of support communications—brochures, ads, audiovisual presentations—and the design of physical facilities such as model installations in showrooms and offices and the special education center were an essential integral part of ensuring the market success of the system. My participation in the task force responsible for designing, developing, producing, and marketing AO2 was critical to the integration of all these aspects of design into the planning and execution of AO2's market launch. Probably the most important design management issue has to do with *the management of corporate resources and the corollary issue of who should manage this broad spectrum of activities*.

The Herman Miller example of the way the design and communications were managed during the period they were my responsibility may not necessarily be the precise model for every company for all time. However, comparing my experience with Herman Miller to that of Philips, I have become convinced that one person in any company, no matter how small or large, or how broad its scope of activities, should maintain the overview perspective for corporate design and communications and hold the portfolio responsibility for it. And, again, that person should be at the top of the echelon of the organizational structure. At Herman Miller, George Nelson held the portfolio in the company's more informally operated days. As the company grew and needed more internal coordination, I held the portfolio as a vice president who reported directly to the president.

At Philips, which will be discussed in detail in Part 3, the portfolio does not actually exist, although during the time when I was managing director of corporate design, my original responsibilities for product and packaging design gradually spilled over into an informal involvement in the general sphere of corporate design and communications. Formalization of this responsibility transfers the management of these corporate resources from a scatter-shot approach to one of strategic advantage to a company.

REFERENCES

1. Charles Eames, "Evolution of a Design," *Progressive Architecture,* November 1962, pp. 140–142.

2. Ibid.

3. Ralph Caplan, *The Design of Herman Miller,* Watson Guptil, New York, 1976, p. 84.

PART THREE

PHILIPS AND DESIGN MANAGEMENT

CHAPTER SIX

Plugging in Design as a Global Strategy

When I arrived at the headquarters of Philips in Eindhoven, the Netherlands, in 1980 as its new managing director of corporate design, the giant Dutch electronics company was being operated as a true multinational. In fact, it was one of the pioneer multinational companies of Europe, with subsidiary organizations in a number of countries before World War II.

Because the Netherlands provided such a small home market, almost from its beginnings in 1891 as a producer of incandescent lamps (light bulbs), Philips ranged across its borders for broader market coverage. The protectionist environment existing before World War II and in the years immediately after, largely at that time as a measure to shield struggling war-shattered industries during their reconstruction, were conditions in which multinationalism had its *raison d'etre*.

Like the very model of the modern Major General of Gilbert and Sullivan fame, who was the epitome of the long arm of colonialism of Victorian Britannia, Philips was the very model of a modern multinational of the industrial expansionism of the first half of this century. The company was studied as a standard Harvest case study of a matrix-structured multinational.

By 1980 Philips had become an industrial giant with a turnover of 36 billion guilders (approximately $18 billion) and was operated with a Dutch benevolence that granted almost complete autonomy to the national organizations (see Figure 6-1). These national organizations operated as fiefdoms with duplicative factories producing coffeemakers, radios, or television sets for local distribution. There was generally a Dutch expatriate managing director of the national organization. In true baronial style, this director often was a figure of power in the adopted country because Philips was a large employer with high product and brand visibility. In many cases the social and commercial integration of Philips into the country culture was so complete that it was not considered a "foreign" company. It was a point of pride among Philips people that most French people, for example, thought Philips was an indigenous company, even pronouncing the name in the French way. In other cases the Philips name was replaced with a national brand name. Until the mid-1980s the Philips name was virtually unknown in the United States, but its brands—Norelco, Magnavox, and Sylvania—were household names.

Figure 6-1. One of the world's huge post–World War II multinationals, Philips transformed itself by 1991 into a leaner, more competitive global company.

This structure had important implications for decision making and product policy responsibilities. In classic matrix fashion, decision making was negotiated between the national organizations and product divisions, with the implicit power lying in the hands of the national organizations. Unifying coordination was only broadly administered by the Board of Management headquartered in Eindhoven and the staff departments providing umbrella services to the product divisions and national headquarters. Concern Industrial Design Center (CIDC), as it was called in 1980, was one of those "staff services."

DESIGN AS A COTTAGE INDUSTRY AROUND THE WORLD

When I took up my duties at Philips I was confronted with a design organization trying to deal with this complex and far-flung infrastructure of duplicative production activities and the minuet of decision making between product divisions and national organizations regarding product planning and development. Brazilian factories were producing Brazilian-designed blenders for Brazilians; English factories were producing English-designed television sets for the U.K. market; U.S. factories were producing coffeemakers for the U.S. market.

In all there were 14 product divisions, which between them made just about anything that could be plugged into an electrical outlet. The product scope for which our designers were responsible included personal care products; small domestic appliances; major domestic appliances; consumer electronics, which included radios, hi-fi, television, video recorders, car radios, and later, compact disc players; lighting, ranging from light bulbs to large industrial lighting fixtures; telecommunications; data systems; medical systems; testing and measuring instruments; and large-scale communications control installations (see Figure 6-2). In addition to product design responsibility for this breathtaking

Figure 6-2. The scope of Philips electrical and electronic products in 1980 was the broadest of any company in the world. A "Philips face" to its product designs was difficult to discern.

range of diverse products, CIDC was also responsible for the graphics and packaging of all products.

The communications contacts for this vast and sprawling spread of products were further complicated by the shared decision-making tasks, not only between the product divisions and national organizations but within each of these entities. Each product division had a commercial director and a technical director. And the national organizations' operations were in the hands of a commercial, technical, and financial management triumvirate. As an American accustomed to a hierarchical structure and clear lines of authority, I confronted the Philips matrix (maze!) at first with disbelief but also with determination to find some way through the maze to improve the design quality of Philips' products. I had taken the design management position based on my conviction that Dr. Wisse Dekker, then executive vice president of the Board of Management, was prepared to lead the company through a dramatic restructuring when, as it was expected, he stepped into the presidency. The challenge of redirecting a design organization of the scope and complexity of CIDC was too interesting to refuse.

REDESIGNING THE DESIGN ORGANIZATION

My first task was to deal with the problems of CIDC itself. Philips had a well-established design organization which had its genesis in 1928 under the direction of an advertising department called the Propaganda & Art Center. The department was headed by architect Louis Kalff. This development was rather visionary in that it attempted to bring under one umbrella the design of advertisements, brochures, and other promotional materials; the design of exhibitions and displays; and the coordination of product designs created in the various divisions. Although the product design aspect seems to have been mostly one of somehow adapting visual communications to the designs engineered by product divisions and national organizations, a rudimentary corporate identity program existed.

The evolution of the industrial design function from these early beginnings proceeded through that of a design group attached to the audio product division to an independent central design organization with a specified corporate task under the direction of Rein Veersema, the second director of design. The inclusion of product design in the development process made considerable progress under Veersema, and his attempt to articulate a corporate design policy for Philips contributed to the formalization of a design program.

Knut Yran was appointed to the post of director of design in 1966; the importance of the design function at Philips was firmly established under his fervent and often flamboyant leadership. Yran was a painter and poet who had established a reputation as a designer, especially in the design of luxury ocean cruise liners, which was an important industry in his native country of Norway. He was a key figure of his generation of "star" designers, which I characterize as the first wave of industrial design professionalism. Along with Norman Bel

Geddes and Raymond Loewy, who Yran greatly admired, these designers were primarily concerned with style and appearance. Though Yran frequently exhorted his Philips designers to realize that design is more problem solving than artistry and even developed a "design track" to specify the methodology of the design process, his ambivalence about such a process philosophy was evident in the emphasis he placed on presentation style and skills. Typical of his generation, he had a penchant for futuristic, Darth Vaderesque imagery, apparent in both the advanced product research concepts he presented to commissioners and in the stylistic, artfully rendered presentations for the bread-and-butter product lines. His style of operation also reflected a fascination with science fiction wizardry and its connection to a modernist way of thinking and doing things. Designers under his direction recall with both humor and frustration the weekly meetings during which products were placed on a turntable in the center of a specially designed conference table. Yran sat at the head of the table with a custom-designed control panel at his fingertips to spotlight the product model and manipulate a remote TV for detail inspection. The visual critique was accompanied by a checkpoint audit of the design track procedure and timetables.

The evaluation process established a disciplined methodology, but there were several difficulties. First, the sheer number of products to be reviewed resulted in time inefficiency and arbitrary decisions. Second, the evaluation subjectivity, despite attempts to establish objectivity into the design process, created a director authority that had a tendency to stifle both creativity and the development of management capabilities and decision-making confidence among the designers.

Nevertheless, Yran elevated the cause of design at Philips. He achieved a status that was formalized in the establishment of a direct reporting and communication link to the Board of Management.

The design group expanded significantly in size during Yran's tenure, reaching over 200 designers by the time of his retirement in 1980. John Heskett in his book about design at Philips, states, "Ultimately, the considerable growth of CIDC under his leadership, the extension of its role in Philips, and the acceptance of it as a necessary element in overall strategic policy, must be seen as positive achievements which laid a foundation for the further developments of recent years."[1]

However, Heskett also identifies one of the crucial problems that created a major obstacle to both the strategic contribution design could make to Philips and in the qualitative results of design work. Heskett writes:

> ...the organizational plan for CIDC specified a management process with the design group [the design track], but did not identify a pattern of linkage to other functions in the company, and there were still frequent difficulties in relationships with the product divisions. Their managers often continued to regard design as a late, superficial addition to the process of product development and could still impose ideas upon product design, for example, insistence on wood instead of metal for housing. Proselytizing the virtues of design, no matter with how much conviction, was clearly not enough to achieve the fundamental change of attitude needed in this respect.[2]

The organizational ambiguity of the relationship between each product division and the national organization and the fluidity of decision making, which resulted in failure to take responsibility or to "own the problem," was a formidable management challenge.

DESIGN: FROM A COTTAGE INDUSTRY TO A GLOBAL ORGANIZATION

I decided to make a start by reorganizing CIDC to be, first, more capable of producing quality work, and, second, more effective in its relationships with our product division commissioners, regardless of the difficulties involved with that objective. In order to achieve these results, the design process had to be managed. My overarching goal, however, was to prepare the design organization for the macroeconomic changes that were pressuring Philips to restructure itself to make the shift from a multinational to a global company.

In a speech entitled "From a Multinational to a Global Company," presented at Harvard University in 1987, Cornelius van der Klugt, then president of Philips, reviewed the trends in the early 1980s that precipitated a dramatic organizational change. New patterns of competition, he said, "were having a forceful effect on the electronics industry. In particular, the special tactics introduced into the marketplace by the Japanese have dramatically altered whole industries. The focus is now on electronics."[3] Second, he pointed to the development of global markets for products demanding large-scale markets to absorb production and fast payback on the enormously high investment costs in developing of new technologies. A significant presence in Europe, the United States, and southeast Asia is essential to an electronics company, he said. He also noted that "Centers of Competence" for production must be located in the places in the world where experience, skills, and costs combine to create a high level of efficiency and competency. Finally, he referred to the integration of technology into systems of converging consumer and professional applications.

By 1987 Philips had responded to these trends. Manufacturing rationalization closed inefficient factories and designated others as International Production Centers (IPCs) to manufacture designated products for Philips worldwide distribution. A corresponding organizational consolidation reduced the two-headed management of the product divisions to a single senior director. The convergence of technology functions forced an integration of audio and video product division activities and, later, the integration of computer, audio, and video into a home electronics structure.

But perhaps the most far-reaching policy change was that of "tilting the matrix" toward the authority of the product divisions. National organizations were directed by van der Klugt to govern the marketing, sales, and service activities in their countries, but the policy and planning responsibilities for products would be in the hands of the product divisions.

The culture shock to Philips employees was enormous. The decades of power wielded by the national organizations had been eclipsed by the global imperative. As strong and forthright as van der Klugt was, however, his edicts were only slowly taken seriously. Habits entrenched in nearly a century of successful operation could not be expected to change quickly. Some national organizations took several years to abstain from "doing things their way" with regard to product decisions, a situation that continued to cause problems for the design group, although the intensity of such problems gradually diminished.

But this dramatic restructuring had not yet occurred when I joined Philips in 1980. The concept of globalism had still to emerge in strategic thinking at Philips, although some beginning steps to consolidate production were being taken. Designers were scattered around the globe, sitting sometimes singly in factories doing "follow-up" design work, which in actuality meant doing the bidding of product managers or engineers for local-for-local products. There were 104 designers and support staff at CIDC/Eindhoven and 169 designers distributed in some 25 countries. We were decentralized before decentralization hit the management schools several years later as the new flexibility charter for competitive success. But it was decentralization without direction.

The philosophy of Thomas Watson when he was president of IBM seemed applicable to the conduct of the design function at Philips. Watson advocated the strategy of centralizing before a company can successfully decentralize. The groundwork of policy development and organizational coherence has to be laid so that decentralization can work effectively. The eventual goal was to achieve a manageable worldwide design organization whose principal activities would be focused in the three main regions of economic dynamism: Europe, the United States, and southeast Asia. I called my goal the "three-zone strategy" (see Figure 6-3).

To develop a strong core competency for the Philips design program, my efforts would have to be directed to putting a restructured organization in place and establishing a program to improve the quality results of design. The framework for achieving these twin goals was, until I completed my contract agreement as managing director of design for Philips at the end of 1991, a program comprising six major activities:

1. The establishment and maintenance of product design as a managed process, with an organizational structure that is both coherent and compatible with the Philips organizational structure. Evaluating and fine tuning the structure is a continuing process.

2. The formulation of a product design policy on a corporate level that establishes the responsibilities of the design group and serves as a working document for evaluating the quality of design work.

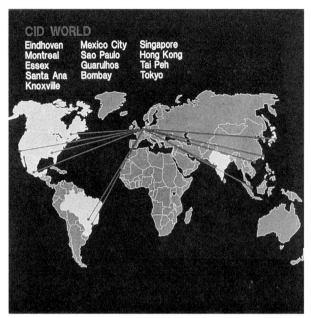

Figure 6-3. The early strategy was to change the Philips design organization to one that was structurally and functionally global.

3. Creating and providing programs for the improvement of professional standards.

4. Utilizing new technologies and techniques to improve design efficiency and quality.

5. Creating programs for harmonization of products, systems, packaging, and graphics to achieve a corporate identity.

6. Improving the product creation process and therefore the quality of its results by seeking ways to ensure the involvement of designers as equal partners with manufacturing and marketing.

LETTING THE DESIGNERS MANAGE

One of the first actions taken to get the restructuring and process renewal moving was to devolve management responsibility from a single director downward. I inherited a structure in which 25 people had reported directly to Yran, a situation that needed to be rapidly changed. With the invaluable advice of deputy director Frans van der Put, who had long years of experience in CIDC and proved to have good insights into the capability potential of the design staff, I appointed a team of design managers whose responsibilities were to manage the design activities of their assigned product division responsibility (see Figure 6-4). At that time the design groups consisted of consumer electronics, professional equipment and systems, light, small domestic appliances, personal care products, and major domestic appliances. Graphics and packaging was also assigned to a design manager. This group of design managers plus the deputy director made up the Design Policy Committee (DPC), which I chaired; each of the 9 committee members reported directly to me, considerably reducing the original number of 25. The committee's function was to ensure that the tasks defined by a design policy, which the committee would together formulate, were carried out at a corporate level. They were responsible for guiding the operational design activities and for participating in the formulation of long-term goals for the Philips design function.

It is interesting to recall that some of those appointed to the first group of the design management team were hesitant to accept the responsibility because of a lack of self-confidence. However, in a very short time, each design manager rose to the challenge of responsibility and proved quite capable of making valuable contributions to the early work of building a managed design organization.

Defining Who Designers Are and What They Do

I assigned two working groups within the DPC to the tasks of developing a design policy and building an organizational structure to enable the design function to deal more effectively with an amorphous but slowly reformulated Philips organization.

The first group produced a design policy draft for consideration by the other members of the DPC. This was an important exercise that not only achieved the policy statement but established the group as a working team and underscored the importance I placed on spreading responsibilities. The design policy, in stating the mission of CIDC, firmly anchors design within the corporate strategy framework by defining CIDC's responsibility as the group with the corporate task for conducting the product design function in the product development process and for overseeing the quality of design of Philips products, product systems, packaging, and graphics worldwide.

The criteria for evaluating design quality are specifically identified in the policy statement. These address the following design quality issues:

1. Is the product ergonomically designed to satisfy human factors? Is it intelligible?

2. Does the product not only meet safety standards, but exceed these by anticipating potential hazards?

3. Does the product successfully satisfy a consumer need?

4. Is it compatible with its environment, including achieving a harmonious coexistence with other Philips products?

5. Is the product designed to utilize materials, production processes, and energy in the most efficient way?

6. Are the aesthetic elements, such as form, colors, textures, as well as graphic information, expressed and integrated in an appropriate manner?

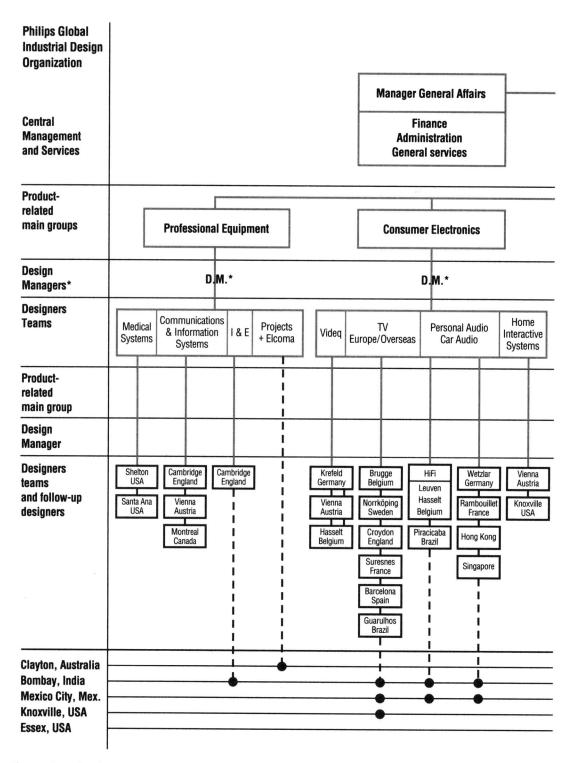

Figure 6-4. The design organization in the early 1980s reflects a significant shift toward the delegation of responsibilities.

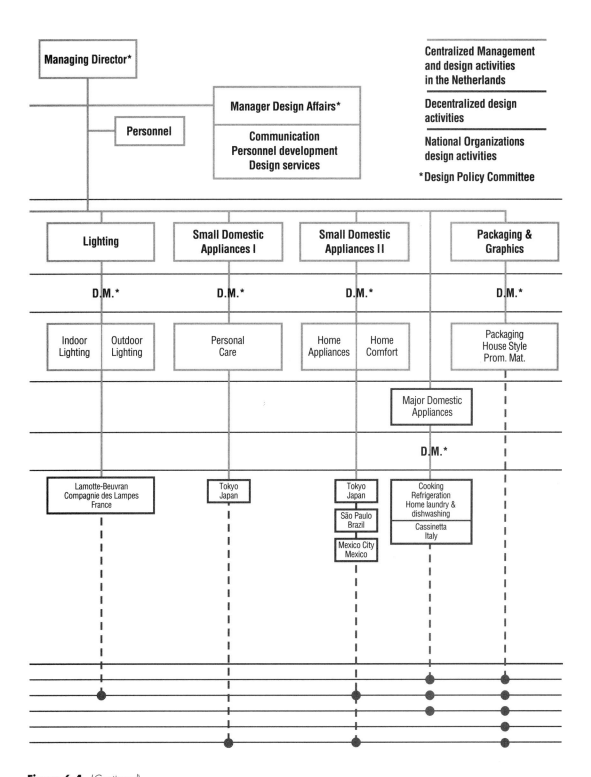

Figure 6-4. (Continued)

Managing the Design Process

The second task force was assigned the work of developing a new structure for CIDC that would help us to get a better grip on our relationships and areas of responsibility with our commissioners and, in some cases, national organization management. The organizational structure should also reflect the first phase of my three-zone strategy for strengthening the core design capability.

This task force called the design organization restructuring the "Renewal Program." Their recommendations went beyond a formalized structure to include career path planning and suggestions for professional development. By 1984, the Renewal Program was launched with a new design organization structure.

The design managers, as the chart (Figure 6-4) indicates, had delegated responsibility for the management of their respective design teams and for the liaison activities with the appropriate people in the product division for which they were responsible. In the case of product graphics and packaging, their work relationships were associated with all product divisions we served and with the relevant product design team for each project.

In a further devolution of responsibility, contact designers were appointed to manage the day-to-day design liaison communications with product division commissioners.

The question of accountability and the management of the design program merits some explanation, especially since attempts to deal with accountability in discussions about design are about as successful as trying to bounce a ball of cotton. How do you measure design effectiveness? How can you assign accountability to design? These are questions that usually wander off into fuzzy theorizing about the subjective aspects of design.

CIDC was established prior to 1980 as a profit and loss center. Its work was derived from commissions by product divisions, who were charged worker-hour fees for design services. Each year CIDC was expected to develop its budget based on projected workloads from commissioners. An additional 35 percent of the income to CIDC was provided from the corporate budget to fund advanced development, management costs, and other overhead expenditures.

My introduction to the CIDC budget process was an enormous budget over-run from the previous year which landed on my desk several days after I was installed as director, a situation no one was very happy about, most especially me. It was obvious that financial accountability needed to be tightened. The 35 percent corporate kick-in appeared to me to be an income source that could be highly vulnerable in the future. I reduced this to 7 percent over the years, which was a worthwhile anticipation, since the subsequent budgetary discipline of Philips would indeed have knocked the pins out from under that source of income. I replaced this coverage of overhead expenses by building them into the per-hour fees charged to commissioners. Guess-work estimates of workloads in developing budgets were also replaced by firm budget commitments for the ensuing year from commissioners, which in turn influenced how we realigned our design teams to meet commissioner demand. Beyond budgetary accountability, however, is the important point that CIDC had to, in effect, sell its services to product divisions. The only way to ensure a corporate direction for product design is to be certain the quality of services is seen to be a cost-value benefit to the buyers of the service. This is the ultimate accountability test for a design manager whose responsibility is to deliver a corporate design program.

Over a few years' time, we were able to increase incrementally the fees we charged commissioners. There was never any outcry. Our workload continued to increase. In 1983 CIDC completed 632 design projects. By 1990 we had completed 1730 with about the same number of designers we had in 1983. The happy conclusion can be drawn that commissioners considered our services worth what we charged; we were no longer drawing off significant funds from the corporate budget; designer productivity had dramatically increased. I think these financial elements provide a valid and concrete evaluation measurement of performance of both the quality of design work and the design management function.

Another accountability measure of the managing director of design was my contract with the Board of Philips. Along with other senior management, I made an annual agreement to accomplish certain very specific objectives. At year's end, accomplishments were checked with objectives. Remuneration was directly tied to the outcome of the contract. I have learned that it is possible to define specific performance and accountability measurements for design management tasks. Many of these, I might add, depend on the cooperation and performance of other people. It was my job to motivate them to achieve our objectives.

IMPROVING PROFESSIONAL STANDARDS

An additional problem facing me in 1980 was the quality of the design talent at CIDC. Although much of the talent was good, too much of it was only fair to mediocre. This situation was, in my opinion, a top priority for correcting.

However, the Dutch social laws made it almost impossible to separate an employee, and the Philips employment-for-life culture reinforced government and union obstacles. However, a companywide overhead value analysis in the early 1980s of all departments conducted by an outside consultant was somewhat helpful. The audit of CIDC redefined some jobs and recommended eliminating others. Those holding redundant jobs in some cases elected to leave. Hiring opportunities became available when we were able to gain some job slots as a result of trimming overseas design operations with the closure of design offices in the United Kingdom, Australia, Sweden, Belgium, and the United States and the consolidation of design groups in the north of Holland and in France. A few years later, Dutch social law changes allowed a retirement option at age $57^1/_2$ to help open up jobs for young people and ease Holland's high unemployment problem. We persuaded some of the affected designers to exercise this option. We were thus able to rejuvenate the design organization with an infusion of fresh talent.

I placed great emphasis on developing active contacts with design schools all over the world, evaluating course content, teaching quality, and student portfolios. This involved maintaining a close relationship with those schools whose programs were of interest to me and relying on professors whose judgment could be trusted to recommend graduate students for job interviews. We also developed a student internship program, which contributes to supporting the quality of design education with work experience as well as provides us an opportunity to screen potential job talent. Students have also accomplished some worthwhile work at Philips. Everyone wins!

I was personally active in our student recruitment program, but these activities were also delegated in a variety of ways. Several of our very good British and Dutch designers, for example, make yearly visits to their former design schools to look over the crop of students. Experienced, satisfied designers are good advertisements for career opportunities for young students.

A recruitment program that includes monitoring design education programs internationally and making personal visits to the most interesting of these, sponsoring internships and student design award programs, participating as jurists for international design competitions and speaking at design conferences, builds visibility for the corporate design program. All these activities are important tasks of design management. The strength of any corporate design activity rests on a strong foundation of the best design talent a manager can assemble.

Part of the problem of the mixed quality level of design talent at CIDC in 1980 was the age level, which was too high. We were too heavily weighted away from the younger designers who are more likely to bring fresh, new thinking to design problems. Designer "burnout," although certainly not applicable to everyone, is still frequent enough to pay attention to in managing the mix of design talent. Eventually, starting from an average designer age of 41 (versus 33 in Japanese Electronics Corporation design departments), we were able to bring our average age down to 32 by 1990. The implications of this are that we had tightened our hiring standards and improved our recruiting program in general.

As an international company, we had too large a concentration of Dutch designers. I found, in addition, there was a two-way "off limits" attitude between CIDC and the respected design department at the Dutch Delft Technical University. Yran considered their graduates too technically oriented, and the students had a disdainful attitude toward CIDC. Even among the predominant Dutch population in our design group, the cream of the design education system was noticeably absent.

I considered an international culture essential to our design program. After all, we were going to move in the direction of a global design structure and activity according to the centralization and decentralization of the three-zone strategy. Over the decade of the 1980s, I was at constant war with the Philips staff personnel department on the issue of hiring non-Dutch designers. Theirs was a bias of national job protection. Mine was a bias toward achieving a corporate design strategy and thus an overall corporate strategy of designing and developing products conceived out of an international cultural approach.

Figure 6-5. Corporate Industrial Design had become global in its structure, function, and culture, with 21 nationalities represented on staff.

By 1990 CID, as it was renamed (Corporate Industrial Design), was populated by designers representing 21 nationalities (see Figure 6-5). Of those who were Dutch, a large number were graduates of the Delft Technical University; we had made a concerted effort to woo the interest of the excellently educated, technologically attuned graduates.

Raising the level of professionalism is an ongoing design management task even when you are building on the base of an acceptable talent level. For CIDC in 1980 a crash program was indicated. In addition to the measures already described, a series of seminars called "Interdesign" were instituted to bring our designers into contact with the thinking of leading design practitioners.

We also conducted hands-on workshops to upgrade design skills. International designers Katherine McCoy and Michael McCoy, Klaus Krippendorf, Reinhart Buter, Charles Mauro, Niels Diffrient, James Woudhuysen, Bill Plumb, Bruce and Susan Burdick, Santiago Miranda and Perry King, Bill Moggridge, John Rheinfrank, and a stream of people from Fitch, Richardson Smith were among the people I brought in to focus on application of theories in packaging and product graphics, ergonomics, user interface, and product semantics. Katherine McCoy and Michael McCoy, who cochair the design department at Cranbrook Academy and maintain practices in graphic and product design, spent six months as designers-in-residence, working closely with graphics and product designers.

Giving Designers the Tools They Need

Closely associated to these efforts to improve the level of professionalism is the provision of tools and techniques to upgrade the quality of design work and improve productivity. Following two visits to CID by the American industrial designer Niels Diffrient, who worked with us on his ideas about human engineering, we grew increasingly convinced that we needed to build a competency in this area both for broad application throughout Philips' engineering groups and within CID. After discussions with engineering departments in various product divisions, the consensus was that efforts to build competency in human engineering or ergonomics should be centralized within CID. We were selected to build and manage this activity because it was acknowledged that CID with its corporate responsibility for the visual image of all products and packaging is the vital connector between product divisions.

Building on work already done by the Institute for Perception Research, which is a joint project between Philips basic research group and the Eindhoven University of Technology for conducting human engineering research and supplying consultant services to product divisions and CID, the new human factors group would be a full-time staff supplying expertise to CID and product engineering groups. The growing area of man-machine interface for professional and semiprofessional users as well as nontrained users in home electronic products required specialized skills. The program was launched in 1986 with a user interface workshop for 28 CID designers.

The demand for trained ergonomists to supply the expertise has increased to the extent that by 1990 there were seven on CID staff. They consult on design projects as team members on an as-needed basis and frequently participate in workshops for product creation. Their scope of specialization includes user needs analysis, usability specifications, interaction design, early prototyping, and evaluation. The whole area of interaction design for technically complex equipment has created a need for industrial designers and graphic artists who are specialists in giving form and intelligibility to defined interaction with electronic products. By the end of 1990 CID had some 25 designers who had competence in interaction design.

Technology support for design tasks in the form of computer-aided design (CAD) has revolutionized design work in just a few short years. The design staff had been working for a number of years with other departments in Philips to identify existing CAD systems and evaluate them against the requirements for our industrial design process. We determined by 1985 in an analysis of the CID industrial design process that existing CAD systems showed two major problems in relationship to our process:

- Three processes (product, product graphics, and packaging design) were mainly sequential and required physical models.

- Long backward loops in the development process resulted from insufficient evaluation tools at the start of the design track.

The CAD study group identified requirements for excellent, highly interactive two-dimensional and three-dimensional capabilities for modeling and human factors evaluation. These capabilities improved evaluation tools, resulting in a more efficient selection of design proposals at the start of the design process.

Evaluation of commercially available CAD/CAM systems led to the conclusion that an industrial design CAD system did not exist. The solution seemed to be to customize a mechanical design system to industrial design needs. Intergraph appeared to have both the best possibility and the most interest in developing with CID a dedicated industrial design CAD system featuring product, product graphics, packaging, and graphics capabilities.

In 1986 an Intergraph Mechanical Design System was installed at CID. A program was established for both the training of designers to use the system and continuation of the development of expanded software programs in cooperation with Intergraph. Although Intergraph was judged as one of the best CAD systems for industrial design tasks, CAD systems can only be fully efficient if there is an interaction and follow-up capability with engineering development and manufacturing. Because Philips uses three different computer systems, industrial design information has to be transferred from one system to another through interfaces. The complexity of product geometry does not allow for faultless interfacing from one system to another. We continue to work with Intergraph to develop software to solve this problem.

In cases where the total process from product concept to creation and realization was carried out with one system (Intergraph with Philips Medical Systems and Unigraphics with domestic appliances) full diffusion of CAD-ID to CAD engineering, and CAM was achieved by 1990.

We have also installed MacIntosh computers in our graphics department. The system's capabilities were tested in doing the design work for our CID newsletter, INFORM. By teaching themselves and experimenting with the layout, photographic, and graphic possibilities to create a visually exciting publication, the designers determined that the system would also greatly expand the design possibilities for their daily graphic design project work.

Team Approach to Stimulating New Thinking

We introduced the concept of workshops early on as a technique for upgrading skills and communicating information. Workshops have also become an important and effective technique for the conceptualization and design of new products.

As a product creation approach, these workshops grew out of working meetings that began in 1984, which I called "DART" (design and research team). Philips designers from various locations in the world attending trade shows, such as the consumer electronics show in Japan, met afterward to compare observations and "intelligence." Discussions of trends and how these would affect Philips product design were compiled in a report for all CID management, designers, and, importantly, product managers.

An evolutionary change in the DART meetings as a result of interest sparked by the designer reportage of the trade shows was to enlarge the meetings to include a collaboration of the designers in developing product concepts from the thinking stimulated by the trade show. Growing interest by our commissioners in the results of these collaborative efforts resulted in their sponsorship and participation in workshops of several days' duration as a technique for communicating project briefs, the immediate development of concepts by several teams of designers, and presentation to the commissioners. In some cases concept models are speedily converted to production models following workshops. In other cases, concepts are integrated into a long-range product development plan.

Workshops are now a way of work life at CID. But there have been many variations on the basic purpose and conduct of the workshops. Sometimes the emphasis is on design research, as was the case in launching our youth-directed consumer electronics products (described in a case study). Other workshops have been commissioned by business units to explore application of a new technology to products, as in the case of the office lighting of the 1990s workshop (see Figure 6-6). In this case, the lighting product division gave CID a brief to research trends in lighting in the office environment and develop product concepts which would utilize new lighting technology developed by Philips. The CID lighting design group brought in six consultant designers from Europe and

Figure 6-6. Workshops are a technique for developing concepts and involving commissioners. Workshops are also forums for stimulating cross-fertilization of ideas among designers who do not normally work together, and with consultants, as in the case of this workshop to develop a new lighting range.

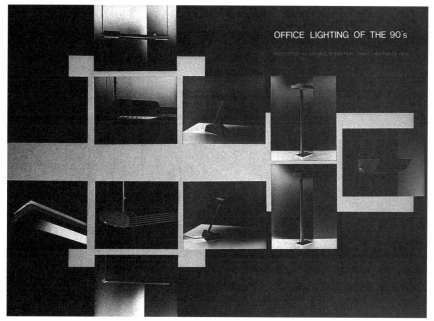

OFFICE LIGHTING OF THE 90's

Figure 6-7. The lighting product division had a new technology but no ideas about how to apply it. Corporate Industrial Design Light group designed the office lighting of the 1990s range for a complete lighting system for offices.

the United States to work with them during a week-long workshop. At the workshop's conclusion two complete ranges of integrated office lighting systems were presented to the commissioners. The conceptualizations were so well formulated that both were accepted for further development and production (see Figure 6-7). These are just two examples of workshops that have provided the impulse for completely new product lines for Philips in contrast to workshops for designing a new generation of products.

This work technique also encourages cross-fertilization of ideas and thinking well beyond the day-to-day task work. Designers from various groups and world locations are brought together, stirring the pot of creativity both in terms of different professional approaches and in the cultural diversity that is now characteristic of CID. Designers say workshops give them a chance to work in product areas outside their area of responsibility and have contact with designers with whom they do not normally work. A successful variation on the CID staff workshops is the importation of design consultants to join in the participation. They may direct the workshop, act as a resource, or join in as team members with CID designers in concept development. Consultants may also form their own teams in a quasi-competition with CID designers. These variations and their results will be described more fully in the case studies.

As a technique for raising the quality level of design work, this process has many positive impacts: dialogue with commissioners, peer stimulation (and competition!), exposure to new information, anchoring of the decentralized design groups to CID policies and directions, and providing opportunities for creative "jolts" to relieve the sameness of day-to-day tasks. Work methodology and workshops have become synonymous at CID. Commissioners are so satisfied with the results that they are happy to finance the costs.

CREATING A CORPORATE IDENTITY

One of the most visible symptoms of the Philips former multinational style of operation in which national autonomy ruled the day was the vast visual melange of products. With all the national organization and product managers doing their own things, the visual quality of products varied from reasonably good to very bad. The most consistent characteristic of Philips products was their inconsistency.

Angela Dumas and Alan Whitfield, in a design management seminar paper for the London Business School, discuss what they call the "silent designers" of corporations: the engineers and marketers who "unknowingly participate in design tasks" scattered throughout the company.[4] The engineers and marketers at Philips were not-so-silent designers. They knowingly took command of design tasks during the multinational days of Philips.

My strategy for appropriating the rightful corporate role for design and gathering control of the situation with a centralized direction was to give top priority to a harmonization program. It was also my first programmatic step toward improving the quality level of the design of Philips products.

In Chapter 7, the case study on harmonization describes its purposes, how it has been organized, and its impact on the design quality and corporate identity for Philips products. If I were to cite the single most far-ranging design management accomplishment for Philips during the 1980s, the harmonization program would have to stand as the strongest design influence on the company.

DOES THE DESIGN PROCESS HAVE TO BE MESSY?

John Thackera, in a review of Peter Gorb's book, *Design Management: Papers from the London Business School,* comments that design consultants learned to their dismay during the 1980s boom of design consultancies that "the crucial business of implementation, whether of a corporate identity, or a new product range entailed complex and messy processes and involved people and organizational matters, not just the rational production of a manual."[5]

I could not agree more that design processes are often messy and complex, with multiple considerations going beyond the specific project in question. However, I am more optimistic than Thackera that a rational approach can help bring order out of chaos. Discipline can be applied to the design process that can be understood by marketers and engineers if it is in their interests to adhere to the discipline. The Philips harmonization program has, over a period of 10 years, been understood and accepted as such a discipline. It is an entrenched part of the product creation process and has gradually spread across the borders to other product divisions from its originally targeted professional products group. But of course you don't just write a manual or set of rules and hope everyone will be good scouts and obey. As the harmonization program case study points out, design harmonization is a long process requiring patience and persuasion. And finally, the responsibility for its success must be spread beyond the design manager as a police officer. This has been the case at Philips.

The total corporate identity of Philips, which goes beyond responsibility for products and packaging design, however, has yet to be brought under coherent management. As a result, responsibilities for advertising, public relations, product literature, and promotional materials are decentralized and scattered throughout the product divisions and national organizations. A coherent approach to marketing Philips products as part of a managed corporate identity program is currently on the table. A corporate identity task force was appointed by President Jan Timmer in late 1991 to study this issue and make recommendations for action.

I inherited a house style program, which in 1980 was defined in a manual of great heft and long lists of rules. These included rules for all printed materials, stationery, advertising, vehicles, buildings, and interior signage. There was a House Style Council appointed by the board of management with representatives from CIDC, Patents and Trademarks, and Corporate Standardization and chaired by Corporate Planning and Marketing Services. The manual they had created set forth rules in such complexity and with so many variations that the confusion encouraged ignoring the rules completely. The Council devoted most of its energy to policing the house style. Shortly after my arrival at Philips I became chairman of the Council. My first act was to have a complete audit made of all printed material worldwide, business cards, stationery, brochures, packaging, and advertising. The materials were obtained and displayed in a "War Room" in CID it was apparent that for every rule there were dozens of variations.

This situation was carefully analyzed by a new team, a working committee made up of middle management from the respective areas which reported to the House Style Council. We then formulated a new and simpler program that consisted of six basic rules and three additional rules for very large housemarks (see Figure 6-8).

Jan Timmer, who at the time was responsible for corporate communications and advertising as well as consumer electronics, and his marketing director, Just Veeneklaas, were invited to CID to view examples of the Philips corporate image. They were shocked by the *rotzooi* (Dutch for *mess*) they saw. We then presented our proposed solution, which had been languishing due to a budget crunch. Timmer gave the go-ahead to the budget and gave his full support to the new, simplified corporate identity manual. People were appointed within product divisions, national organizations, and staff departments to implement this

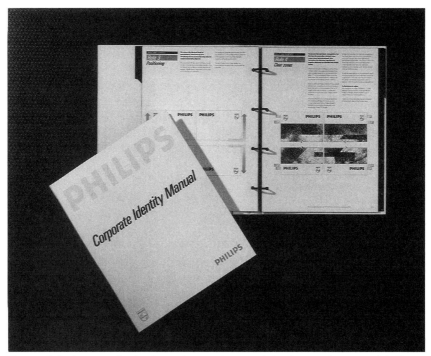

Figure 6-8. A strategy for developing house style manuals that have a chance to work: Keep it simple.

new program in their own areas. The goal was to have it completely implemented by 1991, Philips one hundredth anniversary.

Although compliance was mostly achieved, there were still pockets of resistance, particularly by national organization advertising agencies who felt the rules inhibited their creativity. This was mostly smoke screening, because time after time we could prove that the system did not inhibit creativity.

This does not mean that there cannot be delegated responsibilities for specific areas of activity. There can and should be such dispersal of responsibilities. However, the process has to be managed with an overview for the quality of the design of products, communications, and corporate facilities and an appropriate coherence in verbal communications to the overall image projected by the components of visual design.

Thackera is right. People and organizations (i.e., politics, culture, history) are complex: the design process is messy. This is especially true, it seems to me, in the highly subjective and emotional areas of advertising and other communications and in the design of corporate facilities. But focusing on that messiness begs the question of whether bringing some order out of the chaos is not still worthwhile. The Evoluon case study in the next chapter illustrates that messiness can be eventually transformed to an orderly process.

Managing the chaos of the design process comprises the elements of winning the authority for decision making and gaining the confidence and respect of one's peers in product development, marketing, corporate communications, or facilities management in order to integrate design into a smoothly functioning team process. The issue overarching the requisite authority to act is one that commands almost obsessive attention at design conferences and other venues for discussion of design issues: The status of design in the corporation. Status matters for one reason only. It enables design to be the strategic resource that is so much talked about these days. If design is to be that kind of important element of a company's activities, design must be accepted in the product creation process as equal to the marketing, development, and production functions. As a resource to the total corporate identity of a company, design has to have convincing authority that goes beyond publishing manuals and sitting on advisory committees. Designers should be directly involved with the decision-making responsibilities and the execution of all corporate identity activities.

In the workday milieu, the design director cannot constantly call in the president or executive vice president to fend off the bullies. This is especially true in large companies. The design manager, once having gained the support of the top executive(s), has to fight his or her own battles. But the most crucial thing is to even have the chance to be in the fray. As Peter Sellers demonstrated in his unforgettable role of Chauncy in the film *Being There,* just being there is half the ball game. But the other half makes the difference: The design director has to earn the status for design that is so earnestly desired. This means taking the offensive for design in the company. Of the six tasks I outlined for myself as goals for the design program at Philips, the first five were absolutely not optional if I were to accomplish the last task of winning an equal status in the product creation process. Developing a design policy, raising professional standards, designing a coherent and efficient organizational structure, providing new techniques and tools and a harmonization program for design were really activities for positioning design at Philips on the starting line. These tasks defined all the initiatives that needed to be taken to let everyone else in the company know the design group had all these good things to offer. These tasks involved networking and communications about the design group in creative ways. It meant finding the opportunities for doing nontraditional design activities (see case studies on a youth task force, the design-for-market program, and product planning for lighting in Chapter 7). In short, building status for design meant being a visible and persistent champion for design.

SEPARATING THE EGG WITHOUT PIERCING THE YOLK

Midway during my tenure at CID, it seemed to be the right time for a name change from Concern Industrial Design Center (CIDC) to Corporate Industrial

Design. The new name was more than just an updating to eliminate the dusty word *concern* (Dutch for corporation). More important, it was symbolic of the progress of developing a global design structure. Dropping the center designation in the name allowed for full-fledged design activities to be carried out at Philips' centers of competence (production centers for world distribution of Philips products).

The difference from the situation in 1980 would be that a CID global structure would mirror the structural changes taking place in Philips worldwide. Centralization of design activities in Eindhoven in order to work in close synchronization with each of the product divisions (which were moving toward full responsibility for product policy making) had been the first step in developing a global design structure (remember Tom Watson's "You have to centralize before you can decentralize"). In the years immediately ahead, CID would be ready to manage an effective decentralized, global design program. The centralized core of CID was now in a position to give coherence to all aspects of design activities, to set strategic directions for design that would be in complete accord with our product division commissioners, and to provide central services, which were becoming increasingly sophisticated in their requirements.

The centralization and decentralization concept was basic to the three-zone strategy, which received the blessings of the Board of Management in 1983. The strategy would move forward by first concentrating our efforts in strengthening the European organization with a longer-range goal to integrate southeast Asia and North America into the strategy (decentralization). By early 1989 three centers of competence for design existed in Europe: Eindhoven, the Netherlands, for consumer electronics, professional products, lighting, and packaging; Groningen, the Netherlands, for domestic appliances and personal care products; Cassinetta, Italy, for major domestic appliances. By the end of 1989, the major domestic appliance management responsibility and thus the design responsibility was handed over to the Philips joint venture partner, Whirlpool.

Decentralized design activities in Europe were being carried out under the direction of CID in Hasselt and Brugges, Belgium; Rambouillet, Suresnes and Lamotte-Beuvron and Dreux, France; Wetzlar, Germany; Vienna and Klagenfurt, Austria; and Monza, Italy.

Centralization and decentralization in southeast Asia and North America were beginning to form, although each region was in only the initial stages of developing strong centers of competency. The design team at Philips Marantz Japan, Inc., in Tokyo had delegated responsibility to design certain consumer electronics products for Japan and for export. The design group was Japanese but worked with a CID expatriate who provided strong direction as liaison from Eindhoven. Other design groups under direct CID management functioned in Singapore, Hong Kong, and Taiwan. A majority of Philips USA products were designed by CID in Europe. The Philips consumer electronics products, Magnavox and Sylvania televisions, were designed by the design team in Knoxville.

To conform to a more sophisticated global organization, the Design Policy Committee worked with me to develop a new, more efficient management structure. We still referred to these deliberations as our "renewal program," implying that organizational change, like renewal, is an ongoing process.

The major change was to flatten the organization (see Figure 6-9). Fewer people reported to me, and the new top management team now consisted of only five people—half the previous number. But the second layer of midlevel managers of design managers, who had the day-to-day responsibility for their teams, had been expanded. This group was to meet with the director and the management team at least four times a year in an advisory capacity. The design managers were also responsible for organizing periodic product reviews with the management team.

This organizational structure was in place and functioning well at the time of my planned departure at the end of 1991. The management group was demonstrating confidence and maturity in its approach to problem solving. The structure and process seemed tested and seasoned. The design function at Philips stood ready to make a strong contribution to the challenges Philips would face in a tumultuous 1990s decade.

REFERENCES

1. John Heskett, *Philips: A Study of the Corporate Management of Design,* Trefoil Publications, London, 1989, p. 32.

2. Ibid, p. 25.

3. Cor van der Klugt, "From a Multinational to a Global Company," case study presented at Harvard University Graduate School of Business Administration, 1987.

4. Angela Dumas and Alan Whitfield, "Why Design Is Difficult to Manage," Design Management Seminar Papers, London Business School, 1988.

5. John Thackera, "Design Managers Analyzed," *RSA Journal,* vol. CXXXVIII, no. 5412, November 1990, London, pp. 870–871.

Philips Corporate Industrial Design Organization: Main Functions and Locations

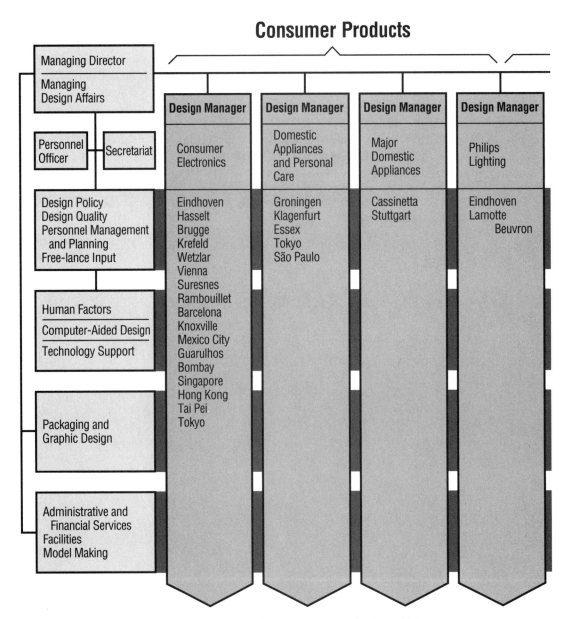

Figure 6-9. Further flattening the Corporate Industrial Design structure in the late 1980s to broaden delegated responsibilities and accommodate decentralization.

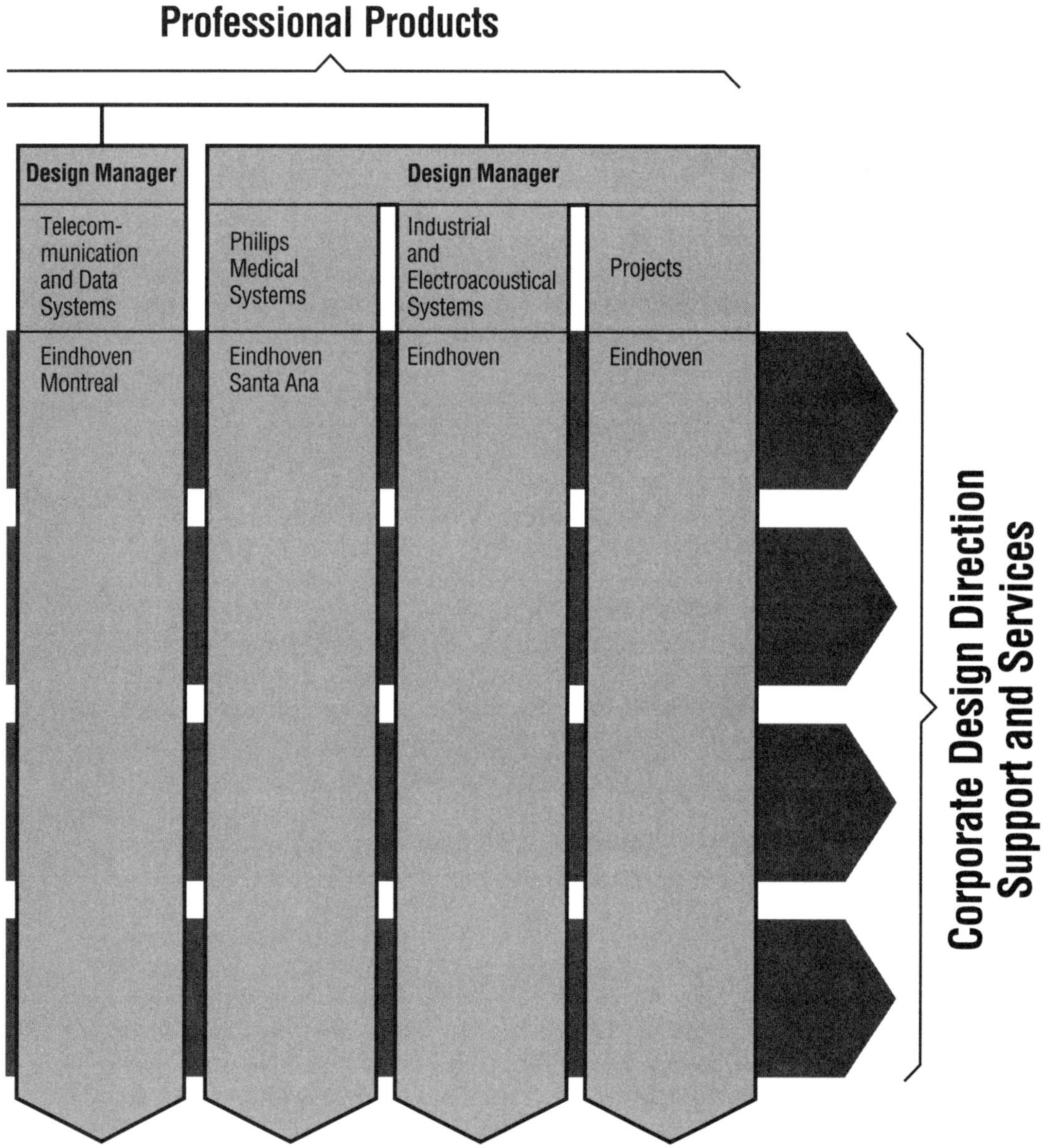

Professional Products

Design Manager	Design Manager		
Telecommunication and Data Systems	Philips Medical Systems	Industrial and Electroacoustical Systems	Projects
Eindhoven Montreal	Eindhoven Santa Ana	Eindhoven	Eindhoven

Corporate Design Direction
Support and Services

Figure 6-9. *(Continued)*

CHAPTER SEVEN

Philips Case Studies and Design Management Issues

CASE STUDY: HARMONIZATION PROGRAM

The lack of any sort of visual unity of Philips products in the beginning of the 1980s was clearly a place to make a start in improving the overall quality of design. A designer of professional products had attempted to persuade the professional group's product managers that this issue was important, but the border rigidity between business groups encouraged attitudes of "I'll do things my way in my product area and I want my products to look different, thank you very much."

Shortly after my arrival at Philips I went to see Gerrit Jeelof, the Board of Management member who held the professional products portfolio. I called his attention to the problem with slides clearly illustrating the dissimilarity in product design, a by-product of which was an uneven level of quality in design concepts and execution. This situation was especially acute because many of the products were used in the same office or health environment, creating a poor overall image for Philips professional products. It made us look decidedly unprofessional.

I asked Jeelof to help me to "educate" the professional products management to the problem by calling and chairing a meeting of the top managers of the division. I would then make my pitch about the problem and how I proposed to solve it.

Jeelof agreed, and the meeting was held. It seemed wise to avoid the term "standardization," since by this time I had learned that the very connotation was anathema to the Philips culture. Instead I built my case around the concept of harmony, describing each business unit as an important instrument in the symphony—an instrument that could be a soloist but, when participating in the efforts to create a symphonic performance, needed to blend with other players. This ideal harmonization needed a conductor to direct the music score which everyone played at the same time.

The case was further made that the practice of designers and commercial and technical people working separately in each product area to create a product's own market image was rapidly becoming outdated as individual products converged into systems in the environment in which they were being used. The rapid miniaturization of electronics was also demanding a rethinking of the visual presentation of professional products. We were, for all these reasons, at a point at which long-range product planning required us to consider these developments as both a necessity and an opportunity to make sweeping changes in the concepts of products and the process by which we would develop them. Both concept and process would be driven by a system approach.

At the end of the meeting, it was agreed that a "harmonization" steering committee would be formed consisting of representatives from the professional equipment divisions, which at that time totaled five separate divisions, and also from Corporate Standardization and Corporate Industrial Design (CID). I chaired the committee. The argument for the necessity of visual coherence as a partner in the technological evolution of products converging as systems won the day.

The steering committee was a working committee. It met often during the critical formulation period of the harmonization program in order to generate proposals for the consideration of the top management interproduct division (professional) committee, specially formed for the harmonization program review and consideration. Huug Sterkenburg, the design manager for professional products, was key to the day-to-day coordination of the steering committee in developing the program.

The goals of the harmonization program were defined and remain today to develop policies to address (1) international market requirements; (2) differing product range life spans; (3) the projection of the Philips image in professional products as one that is contemporary and evolutionary and that maintains continuity; and (4) the achievement of production efficiencies through the standardization of product elements.

The harmonization program for professional products proceeded quite satisfactorily (see Figure 7-1). By 1984 we had achieved agreement on the elements and characteristics to be included in the program and were then able to incorporate these into two manuals for use by everyone in any way involved in design, development, production, and marketing (including packaging and visual presentations in advertising and exhibitions). The first volume of the manual defines those visual elements which were to be strictly followed by using only the explicit specifications set forth in the manual. The second volume provides guidelines for the visual characteristics which are less able because of differing product functions to be confined to strict formulations.

Cooperation with executing the program was good, but the first critical test of the program came when CID felt it had to make sweeping changes in the color program for professional products. The market trends in visual presentation threatened to leave the Philips beige, mushroom, and brown color range behind in outdated decline if we did not anticipate the trends with a complete color range redefinition. The challenge for CID was to argue for flexibility to adapt to change in the conduct of our harmonization program without undermining the principles of continuity, coherence, and compliance.

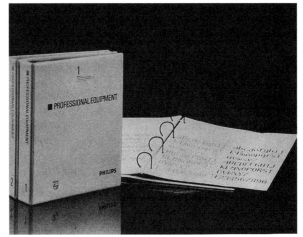

Figure 7-1. The harmonization program brought the array of visually fragmented products into a coherent expression of the family of Philips professional products and systems.

The color change debate was not an easy one. CID argued that our proposals were based on condition changes in lifestyles and approaches to work; new design trends in architecture and interior design; convergence of professional and consumer products in their function and use; changed market requirements; a different Philips organization (consolidation) of product divisions. In addition to these factors we made a case for the new importance of color in its functional aspects. Color accents had been studied in CID for the assistance they give for quick recognition of functions by users. Across a range of products coming together in the same environment, color accents consistently used for the same functions can greatly contribute to user ease and effectiveness in operating equipment.

The professional product division's reluctance to make such a dramatic change centered on production change costs and the difficulties of introducing new products very different from previous generations, a process which could take some years owing to the long development cycles of many products. Less discussed, although most certainly a factor, was a subjective resistance to change from a "comfortable" known color to a range that was dramatically different. What was the greater risk? To trust the design analysis of the situation and make the change/investment? Or was it a greater risk to refute the multiple signals of change and stay with what is known?

We were able to get agreement to the new color program in 1988 for a 1989 launch largely because CID had done its homework in researching the trends in architectural and interior environment changes in offices and commercial and industrial buildings and the trends in consumer and professional electronic products and their new uses and users. We had also studied the design and color directions of our competitors. Based on our investigations we developed a color definition system in order to specify with precision the colors to be used for Philips professional products worldwide. The range from dark grey to light grey with a complementary palette of soft accent colors to choose from offered wide choice and flexibility.

Business units of the telecommunications and data systems group were the first to implement the program followed later by the medical systems and industrial electronics groups. The most important design advantage of the new color program was the flexibility it provided in user interface, screen graphics, textured surfaces, and color use for function, control, and visual differentiation.

The success of the professional products harmonization program has had a positive influence on other Philips product areas. The domestic appliance managing director was quick to see the advantage of a family coherence in household appliances. A committee for harmonization was formed in that product division and functioned similarly to that of the professional products division. Harmonization also migrated from the packaging design programs of professional products to domestic appliances and consumer electronics (see Figure 7-2).

In a recent trend, harmonization is beginning to be applied in the design approach to lighting products, although this is more the result of designer initiative than a managed harmonization program. But of course, for the foot draggers, gradualism succeeds where a cold turkey policy commitment would meet resistance.

An interesting development growing out of the harmonization program was the introduction of a product system that put Philips in a new business. Having had many years of experience in the commercial and office furniture and equipment business, I clearly identified a lack of furniture systems that were truly designed to support electronic office equipment. It seemed to me that an obvious extension of Philips' involvement in automated office equipment should be

Figure 7-2. Philips domestic appliances and consumer electronics products and packaging took their cue from the professional products harmonization program.

to provide support structures that would give complete coherency to a Philips installation. Such a support system should address ergonomic issues of work stations and be adaptive to electronic equipment and not the least of the unsolved problems presented by computers, faxes, printers, and other tools of the electronic office: the spaghetti maze of cables.

I headed a team of designers that included consultants Michael McCoy from the United States, Werner Schultze-Bahr from Germany, and a CID designer, Johnny Lippinkhof. The resulting Philips Electronic Office System (PEOS) solves the cable management problem with vertical and horizontal channels, enabling connection to floor, wall, or ceiling outlets as well as linkage to form a continuous network of connecting configurations of work surfaces (see Figure 7-3). The unique concept of the system is the dual level of the channel accommodation, which also serves as the work unit supports, with the vertical channels carrying cables to equipment such as word processors and computers and the horizontal channels carrying power to other work stations and to peripheral equipment such as telephones and printers, which are not needed at work surface height. A number of accessories, including lighting, were designed as well as storage components and panels for installations in banks and other specialized environments. PEOS offers a turnkey system of Philips professional products to customers seeing the advantages of a completely harmonized system.

The harmonization program remains a solid centerpiece of the design program at Philips, having proved its adaptability to change while providing a framework for design executions that will be compatible with other Philips products and contribute to more consistent quality results. Most important, the development of the harmonization program provided common ground on which CID and the product divisions could build a program of visual unity. The process was also a valuable experience that created a basis for building mutual confidence and cooperation and opening up opportunities for extensions for teamwork between CID and our commissioners in all aspects of the product creation process.

Figure 7-3. The Philips Electronic Office System (PEOS) extends the concept of harmonization by supplying a "support system" that is visually and functionally compatible with Philips professional products.

THE HARMONIZATION PROGRAM
AND DESIGN MANAGEMENT ISSUES

This program was a way to get started at Philips to try to bring some visual unity to the sprawling bazaar of products and to get a handle on quality improvement. Overarching these critical goals was the urgency to bring management to the design process.

The goals I fashioned to appeal to the professional product management had to do with marketing strategies and production efficiencies (certainly legitimate and important goals). If I had, instead, preached a message of aesthetic quality aspirations and pleaded for a corporate visual unity, the harmonization effort would have remained where I found it in 1980—nowhere. By directing the program to the known interests of the product divisions, the harmonization program was able to deliver not only what they recognized as advantageous but also what they did not initially acknowledge: the importance to corporate identity of visually coherent products and the visual quality improvement that was needed.

Thus the harmonization program, now operating as an accepted part of the product creation process, *achieves multiple strategic goals* for Philips in production, marketing, and corporate identity. These are now widely acknowledged achievements.

My own agenda was to use the harmonization program as the *driving force for design quality improvement,* an agenda I knew would not stir the hearts of my Dutch associates. Once quality was obviously improved, I could point to "before" and "after" results. Abstract arguments are not easily bought by non-designers.

The harmonization program was a *design-led program innovation* at Philips that was managed and continues to be managed by CID. But finding a way of "being there" to lead and manage the effort required a "godfather," especially since I was the new boy on the block at Philips and did not have time to wait for a decade of networking my way into the confidence of my management peers. The top-level support was provided by Mr. Jeelof, who gave his *status blessing* to the concept of harmonization. By the time I left Philips in 1991, CID had forged its own status so that design-led initiatives could be launched by CID on its own. Our track record had earned respect.

Taken as a whole, the harmonization program, which eventually reached into all the Philips product divisions, is, in my opinion, as pure an example of managing design to achieve corporate strategies as one can find.

CASE STUDY: DESIGN FOR MARKET

The most vexing issue for designers everywhere is that of achieving and maintaining an equal status in the teaming process of product creation. The situation of the relative influence of the designer in the product creation process at Philips was also one that was chronically erratic, depending for the most part on the level of sensitivity to the importance of design of each product manager. Even within business units the status was never quo: a good team relationship could disappear with the transfer of the benign product manager to another job. And for better or for worse, frequent job rotation is a much-valued human resource management policy at Philips.

It was a high priority of mine to try to do something that would not just prop up the design relationship on an individual and short-term basis but would institute a fundamental change in the product creation process. CID created the opportunity to address this problem. In the spring of 1985 CID organized and sponsored a two-day seminar on the theme of improving the product creation process (see Figure 7-4). More than 50 development and marketing managers joined 28 designers for the first interdisciplinary seminar ever conducted at Philips on the product creation process. The goal was to find ways to improve cooperation and communication in the development process to stimulate innovation and achieve quality results.

The resource people assembled for the seminar included Peter Lawrence, then director of the Design Management Institute of Boston; Jeffrey Miller, pro-

DESIGN STUDY CAFE DUO

Figure 7-4. The Design for Market seminar organized by Philips Corporate Industrial Design was intended to improve the product creation process and elevate the role of design in that process from "receiver of the brief" to partner in creating the brief. CID designer Lou Beeren drew this cartoon early in the seminar to describe the problem.

fessor and chairman of the Operations Management Department, Boston University School of Management; and Peter Gorb, director of the London School of Business Design Management program (see Figure 7-5). A surprise seminar leader was from Philips. Senior Director Lou Ottens was at that time given a special assignment by the president to develop a program for improving innovation at Philips. He was no doubt astonished to be asked to speak at a design seminar, since in his former management position of technical development in consumer electronics, Ottens, the consummate engineer, had been utterly dismissive of designers as nothing more than cosmeticians. As I had hoped, his participation in the seminar was a real eye opener for him.

After presentations by the resource people, the key issues—how to design a structure and process that ensures the communication, cooperation, and parallel development necessary to achieve speed (a goal introduced by Ottens), innovation, and quality results—were tackled by individual teams, which were evenly distributed with development and marketing managers and designers. The recommendations of each team were presented and discussed, with the overwhelming plea that these be followed through with action. Thus, Ottens had his innovation agenda handed to him. By sponsoring the seminar, and, in effect, controlling the agenda (including design!), the issue of team cooperation and innovation in the product creation process was out on the table under the aegis and initiative of the design group.

Figure 7-5. Resource people who participated in the Design for Market seminar. Left to right: R. Blaich, L. Ottens, J. Miller, P. Lawrence, and P. Gorb.

There is no believer like a reformed sinner. Ottens became a design champion in the product creation process, incorporating it as a key element in a program he launched called "Design for Market" (DFM). As a member of his small advisory committee, he frequently sought my counsel and ideas.

By 1986, the DFM program was in operation. Its objectives were defined as follows:

- To emphasize the integral nature of the product creation process
- To define the keys for building sustainable competitive advantage
- To gain the commitment of management to a staged, coordinated approach to improving the process of product development

The structure of DFM consisted of a series of short seminars with assignments between the sessions for the participating management teams. The seminars combined lectures on concepts and methods, using Harvard Business School case studies as a basis for discussion and study. By the end of the program span of a year, the team's strategic objective for its business unit would be defined, action decided upon, improvement adjustments to the plan taken, and approval of the plan would have been taken by the business unit management. The final step was to review progress and evaluate the results of the DFM process. Seven days in total were spent in seminar session; the team continued to formulate its plans and carry them out at the respective work sites; the team could call upon the assistance of consultants to the program at any time. The program participants were operational teams of line and support staff functions in design, marketing, product and process development, logistics, and manufacturing within business units or product groups.

Materials were developed, and the initial seminar sessions were conducted by Kim Clark, associate professor, Harvard Business School. Because the sessions grew to a number he and his associates were unable to handle because of the time involved, the conduct of the seminars and the materials involved were transferred to a management consultant group, Monitor, with which Clark was associated. Seminar leaders were supplied by both their Boston and London offices.

Earliest support for the DFM came from the consumer electronics and domestic appliance divisions followed by major domestic appliances and medical systems. The component division entered later, but enthusiastically, once the department experienced the program's benefits.

After the program had been in operation for a year, Lou Ottens retired from Philips and I was named DFM Chairman. We transferred the administration duties to a group within the Philips Organization and Efficiency unit.

The program operated a further three years at full throttle. When we approached the point where nearly all relevant personnel had participated, it was agreed that the principles and methodology of DFM had become sufficiently institutionalized in the business units for DFM to be dismantled.

The program made a great difference for the role of design in the product creation process. Designers in nearly all business units are now integrated into the team process and very often are able, at a maximum, to give real leadership to the team (see ROTA '90 case study) or at an acceptable minimum, work on a peer level with team members, negotiating trade-offs to achieve strategic objectives.

DESIGN FOR MARKET AND DESIGN MANAGEMENT ISSUES

By recognizing that the problem of too little meaningful involvement of designers in the product creation process not only was a problem for the design group but also weakened the company's entire product development effort, CID took the leadership in addressing a larger corporate problem, which at the same time could achieve an important goal for the design function. The focus on improving a fundamental *process of strategic importance* to Philips gave legitimacy to this *design-led initiative* and at the same time built respect for the design group. The approach was to address an issue that was in the interests of both the design function and the company as a whole from a business-based point of view, drawing in credible resources from the business world. This was surprising to many of the marketing and production members. It gave them a different perspective about design, which, when coupled with business management principles, was an activity they could understand and appreciate more fully. Capturing their interest meant speaking about design in the language of business and production. These were terms which the marketing and production members understood and respected.

The original seminar and subsequent DFM program raised the *status of design* in the estimation of production and marketing managers when they could appreciate the value of the *design participation on an equal basis* in the product creation process.

As chairman of the advisory committee for the DFM program, my presence and involvement reinforced the design component of the program. My chairmanship for DFM also emphasized the role of design in helping the company to achieve strategic goals—in this case improving the product creation process to attain quality results, improve innovation, and achieve cost benefits.

CASE STUDY: YOUTH TASK FORCE: PRODUCT PLANNING AND DESIGN FOR YOUTH

The new lifeblood injected into CID by adding a significant number of young designers and the international character of these young people encouraged us to think about using their insights and talents in a market segment they were close to: the youth market. A Philips marketing survey for consumer electronics revealed that by the age of 20 brand loyalties are already well established, and, although birth rates in the industrialized world are declining, the youth population group will still represent an important market segment. However, the development of brand loyalty for a lifetime is the critical aspect of crafting a strategic product program for the youth.

The marketing study also had some bad news for Philips. It documented that young people in Europe considered Philips consumer electronics products those that their parents would buy, but young people preferred Japanese products. The image of Philips products as stodgy and uninteresting to young people led Cor van der Klugt, who was then senior managing director for consumer electronics and member of the board, to appoint a youth task force to study the problem and set the course for action.

I served on the task force along with representatives from marketing of several national organizations and consumer electronics division advertising and marketing units. The group headed in the direction of correcting the Philips image by developing an advertising program directed to young people.

After several meetings I requested the opportunity to make a presentation. I began by saying that I thought the task force was starting at the wrong end of the problem. If young people thought Philips products were stodgy, no amount of hip advertising would change that impression if we had the same kind of product designs. We needed to first design and develop products especially for young people and then tailor the advertising and marketing program to the products.

I showed slides of products that had been proposed by CID but which the director of personal audio products had rejected as "unsalable." One of these caught the attention of a personal audio product manager assigned to the task force. He wanted to know why the radio, which he thought was terrific, hadn't been developed. It was vetoed, I explained, by his boss. The product manager, Leo van Leeuwen, responded by proposing that he and CID collaborate to develop it without the blessing of the director.

The radio concept developed up to this point at the initiative of CID had an interesting incubation. One day while passing the work station of a young, recently hired graduate from Kingston Polytechnic in London, I noticed an interesting drawing tacked on his board. The young man, Graham Hinde, explained that the radio design had been his student graduate project. The design was fresh, anticipating the soft forms that would become the design language by decade's end. But above all, it expressed *teens* in every aspect of its visual presentation.

So together, CID and van Leeuwen took commando action to develop the radio cassette recorder. Designer Murray Camens began work to bring the concept into line with the existing cassette recorder mechanism, refining the form and developing the colors (see Figure 7-6). Bob Vranken designed the lively graphics. The product was called the Roller, referring to both the roller skate wheel imagery of the speaker design and to the music connection associated with young people.

When we presented the Roller, by then completely developed, to the senior director of personal audio products, his reaction was predictable. He said he had seen it before. He didn't accept it then and didn't accept it now. Van Leeuwen asked what he should do about the production tools. "Production tools?" roared the director. "You'll never sell that radio." He went further by telling van Leeuwen that he would give him a bottle of champagne if he sold 20,000 (an insultingly low number). "Do I get a bottle of champagne for every 20,000 I sell?" asked the ingenuous van Leeuwen. He pulled out of his pocket an initial order for 70,000, all placed by only three national organizations, Italy, the United Kingdom, and the Netherlands.

Figure 7-6. The Roller is the product that launched Philips into the youth market business.

The quick sellout success on those three markets sent other national organizations running for the bandwagon for what was to become a sales pacesetter and long-running success. The Roller has been celebrated in design award competitions and is still featured in articles about product design trends.

The Roller was also the spark for finally developing a Philips youth program. With the Roller as centerpiece, a full-scale strategy for what was named the "Moving Sound" program was mounted by the personal audio group in collaboration with CID. The program, which was designed to capture the hearts, minds, and lifelong loyalty of young people all over the world, was the first totally coordinated product program. Design was the element driving the highly directed marketing and communications effort; product graphics and packaging design developed by CID were the basis on which all subsequent sales display, advertising, and promotional material were developed (see Figure 7-7). The original Moving Sound design team reflected the global strategy in the international character of its participants. Murray Camens and Cameron Robinson are Australians, Terri Ducay is an American, and Graham Hinde is an Englishman.

From the outset, Moving Sound was also conceived as a long-term strategy in which successive generations of products, promotion, and advertising programs would be launched. Each year a new Moving Sound series would be introduced, just as sportswear and other fashion products present new looks to the fashion-conscious youth. The cumulative impact of promotion from previous generations would have positive benefits not only for the Moving Sound program but for the Philips image in general.

Moving Sound was also a breakthrough for Philips in introducing a coordinated program of promotional materials to national organizations. Cost efficiencies and the benefits of coordinated impact were the themes the personal audio group presented to national organizations.

Moving Sound was in its fifth generation by 1991. Inspired by the success of Moving Sound, the video group decided to embark on a program targeted to children in the 8- to 12-years-old group. Six CID designers were asked to submit concepts for a combined TV and cassette recorder, which were developed to model stage and then submitted to children in several age groups and their parents for reaction in a market test in the United Kingdom. The findings were surprising. All the models, which were perceived as being dramatically different from anything on the market, captured interest because of their design rather than their functions.

More surprising, however, was the clear indication that children reject "childish" color combinations and imagery at a young age. By 8 years of age children show strong preferences for more grown-up, sophisticated designs. The lego-like models were rejected in favor of a spherical TV with a tinted hood and bold black and red colors. Designer Hon Son Lee described the TV design as a "sort of hardware with a software character—a science fiction creature that actually turns out to be a TV set." The market test also showed that multiple features (cassette recorder) were not especially interesting. A remote control was, however, of great appeal.

Figure 7-7. Moving Sound is a global series of audio products whose strategy was to capture youth loyalty for Philips.

Figure 7-8. The Discoverer was the first TV designed specifically for children.

The Discoverer (see Figure 7-8), as the TV was named, was introduced with great success at the Amsterdam Firato (consumer electronics show) in August 1990. It was the hit of the show, and early orders expanded the original production from 20,000 units to 135,000.

The Discoverer was designed and developed as a global product with a cable for satellite connection and common transmission standards. The science fiction imagery is also of universal appeal to children of the preteen age group.

Philips was the first television producer to enter the market with a TV set specifically for children. Hon Son Lee's spherical Discoverer is also a dramatic departure from the box shapes traditionally associated with TV sets. The consumer electronics product division has successfully entered an important market segment (see Figure 7-9).

The domestic appliances and personal care products division also made a significant entry into the youth market with its Tracer shaver for first time shavers and its 16 Ladyshave range for girls (see Figure 7-10). The personal care group was receptive to my suggestion that a shaver developed for the lighter beard characteristic of the Japanese market could be adapted as a shaver for teenage youths who were beginning to shave (a strategy to build an electric shaver habit and a Philips habit simultaneously). The Tracer is a global product and an outstanding success.

It is fair to say that CID was strongly instrumental in, first, leading the company to take an interest in products for young people and, second, forcing the issue with specific design concepts. In all cases, design has marched ahead of the product commissioners in its insistence on innovative visual imagery for

Figure 7-9. The Book and Prophesy are new forms for television to appeal to youthful customers. They were designed to continue the successful momentum established by the Discoverer.

products and a complete program approach to graphics, packaging, and promotional materials. The programs championed by CID for the youth market have all been enormous market successes.

YOUTH PROGRAM AND DESIGN MANAGEMENT ISSUES

The *strategic goal* of targeting the youth market may well have died on the vine if CID had not first planted the seed and then given the struggling seedling a life-saving dose of fertilizer with the Roller. A group of talented young designers was essential to the effort. But the designers may never have had the chance to create their spirited designs if the process had not been managed with a firm

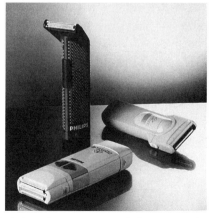

Figure 7-10. Tracer for first time shavers and Ladyshave for young women further segment the youth market.

hand. Initially the key action was taking a strong position with the youth task force. Subsequently, close monitoring of the initial Moving Sound program made sure the principle of coherency from product to promotional materials was achieved.

The youth program is an example of *design-led innovation.* The market success, recognition by design critics, and media interest in the products can, I think, justify thinking of them as innovative. CID contributed to Philips innovation internally by giving strong direction to the idea of spinning off clusters of products from an original concept; of approaching a program in a holistic way, building on the framework of design elements; and of planning from the outset for successive generations of products. These approaches were both *strategic and innovative* for Philips.

The leadership role of CID also helped to reinforce CID not only as an *equal partner in the product creation process* but also as a partner that has the capability of giving leadership in assessing market characteristics and trends and responding to these with successful product designs.

CASE STUDY:
CONSUMER LUMINAIRES

Even though Philips has long held the top ranking in the world for the production of lighting products, the consumer luminaires (home lighting fixtures and lamps) business group has struggled to find a strategy for success. Its tiny 0.2 percent market share, in contrast to its dominant market share in lamps (bulbs) and industrial and commercial lighting, raised serious questions about continuing to remain in this market area when results were so disappointing. The luminaires product management conceded that they failed to understand the nature of the market. Their distribution and marketing efforts were scattered through specialized outlets and audiences that were well outside the mass market distribution of the majority of Philips lighting products. The outside suppliers required because of the relatively small volume production of consumer luminaires were also dispersed because of the dissimilarity between products. As a result, cost prices were excessive.

CID designer Antonio Atjak was assigned the task of working with the luminaires product group. He immediately saw the problem: How could he design successful products if the commissioner was unable to give clear information about what needed to be strategically achieved and for whom the products should be designed?

Atjak began to experiment with some kind of market segmentation model to see if he could on his own bring some clarification to the problem that the luminaire management seemed unable to provide. By chance he attended a seminar sponsored by the Dutch professional design society, Kring Industriele Ontwerpers, during which a presentation was given about a taste matrix research methodology. Atjak recognized he had been thinking in the same direction, but if a model had already been developed and tested, valuable time could be saved by hiring the organization, Bock & Dekker, marketing consultants in Amsterdam, to apply their "Bock Barometer" taste matrix methodology to the luminaire problem.

However, the luminaire product management was unmoved by Atjak's proposal. Without a budget to proceed, Atjak went to the university where he had studied (Technical University Delft), having heard that similar methodologies were being explored by the design department there. It was agreed that the university would supply a student intern to Atjak when "the right student" was identified. After the student arrived from Delft, Atjak put her to work to assemble a taste matrix to classify the Philips luminaires currently on the market. This preliminary exercise was positive, in Atjak's estimation, because it gave the process and his evaluation of it time to mature to a certain level of judgment calls and evaluation before the product managers were involved and could kibitz on the building up of the taste matrix (see Figure 7-11).

After three months' work on the taste matrix, Atjak showed the results to the product manager. The next step, he said, would be to bring in the consultants for an analysis of the taste group to whom Philips should be targeting its products. This was agreed, and Atjak was given the budget he needed to proceed.

Analysis of taste groups, unlike traditional market research, which emphasizes demographic information, is a visual approach to market research. Jay Doblin was perhaps the pioneer conceptualizer of using a matrix analysis for research guidance to the design process. Jay Doblin Associates, now under the direction of Larry Keeley, contend that in today's tough competitive environment, launching products or graphic programs can no longer be casually based on a designer's hunches. These intuitive skills can be channeled more effectively if they are based on strategic information. Careful collecting, analyzing, and presenting such information is the essence of effective, strategic product planning.

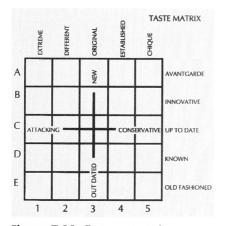
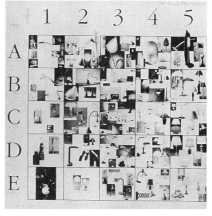

Figure 7-11. Taste matrix studies are an example of one of the new directions in design research.

In the luminaire study, this process was initiated and completely executed by the designer. The resulting product planning credibility depended on a clear and convincing way to present the information to the luminaire product management.

The methodology of the Bock & Dekker Group relies on using 60 to 100 photographs of interiors completely furnished and accessorized, to determine a pattern of preference in tastes of the 1000 people involved in the study. Demographic information is supplied to describe the age, income, educational level of the people in each taste group. The taste groups are then cross-referenced to the Philips products and their assigned position in the taste matrix. A number of manufacturers of products relating to interior design, such as carpeting, floor tiles, window products, and so forth participated as clients in the same study. The taste matrix study is intended to be a continuing process, updating luminaire products within matrix positions with changes indicated by taste group analysis.

The key findings of this program were that the current Philips products were situated in the upper tiers of the matrix and were therefore aimed at a very small potential market. More important, the products in the key matrices where Philips wanted to be were too conservative in their design, even for inexpensive products. A clear indication was given of the products that should be eliminated (those in the outer fringes of the matrix), and the design direction was evident for new products, based on the underlying design assumptions influencing the taste preferences of the market survey participants. The most favorable aspects of the material expression of the products, technical characteristics, and distribution channels could also be deduced from an analysis of the taste matrix.

Armed with all this information, Atjak developed a concept for a range of consumer luminaires that moved from geometric forms to a more amorphic shape, reflecting buyer taste shift to natural, environmentally sympathetic forms. He worked with a supplier to develop a material that expressed a more natural quality (Atjak saw the potential to steer development of new materials when higher-volume potential can make the investment more attractive to the supplier). He also placed a design priority on showing a visual relationship between the lamps, also produced by Philips, and the fixture.

As he became more deeply immersed in the design process, Atjak says he began to see the possibilities for modularity, which provides many more options for variations of models for wider customer choice and at the same time produces manufacturing efficiencies (see Figure 7-12).

The consumer luminaire management was impressed with the design research methodology and the information it provided. However, although they were enthusiastic about the designs for the new lighting range and had initially decided to proceed with it, second thoughts about the radical changes the research prescribed for marketing and distribution caused management to put the entire consumer luminaire product renewal effort on hold. More time was needed to assess the strategic value of consumer luminaires in relation to the overall lighting business.

Figure 7-12. Concept for home lighting resulting from taste matrix research information would take Philips in a completely new direction in this market.

CONSUMER LUMINAIRES AND DESIGN MANAGEMENT ISSUES

This business group and its uncertainties about what its market should be had created strains for several years within our design group in our efforts to try to deal with the commissioners' changing signals. Atjak's initiative in developing his own tool for analyzing Philips' consumer luminaires and in then seeking consultant expertise to supplement and give form to his own design research work was a pure product planning activity.

When we talk about design research and how it has the potential to contribute to product planning, such ideas have a vagueness about them. They sound great, but, what really do they mean? This case study demonstrates one kind of design research and the significant contribution it had the potential to make to product planning for the consumer luminaire group.

The taste matrix is a marketing and product planning tool that can only be creditably developed by designers because they have the aesthetic and cultural basis to make the judgments about matrices positioning. It is therefore design research that feeds knowledge and information into a product planning stage of activity.

Involvement of designers in preproduct planning or design research also focuses designers on target group characteristics and taste preferences. When you are dealing with mass volume products, realities must be taken into account. Rather than blocking them out in favor of "the designer knows best" attitude, designers need to respond to the challenge to reach for the threshold within the range of acceptability.

All the design research and product planning activities described in this case study demonstrate that designers have the capability to work *well beyond the scope of activities* to which designers are normally confined. In this case, the designer didn't take no for an answer when he first proposed the design research project. He was resourceful in using his own skills and experience as well as in finding a way to supplement those. He was skilled at managing the process by recognizing the problem, by finding a methodology to resolve the problem, and by influencing his client to see the value of the methodology.

Design management of this project with its strong emphasis on design research made a significant contribution to clarifying the market segment and appropriate distribution channels with which the consumer luminaire business group had been struggling. The information uncovered by the designer on his own initiative provided the basis for a *rethinking of the strategic value* of this product and ended, as a minimum, the mistargeting of product, customer group, and distribution channels.

CASE STUDY: INTEGRIS C

Following the trail blazed by the design leadership given to the design and development of a new generation of ultrasound equipment, called the Platinum, for Philips Medical Systems (PMS), engineers and product management were receptive to a more prominent role for design in participating in the search for innovative solutions to medical equipment development.

The Platinum project, which has been well documented in John Heskett's book on Philips and the Design Management Institute (Harvard TRIAD Project publication), demonstrated that an alert and talented designer who has tenacity and persuasive capabilities can contribute far more than the usual "design-packaging" tasks to the problem-solving development process. The functional leap forward that the product designer made possible with his truly innovative ideas for the Platinum were rewarded with enthusiastic receptivity by the medical community.

When another designer in our medical systems design group, Gijs Ockeloen, was assigned to the team that includes a product manager, project leader, medical specialist, and engineering manager, to design and develop a successor to the Philips medical systems current line of X-ray stands, the designer was quite clear about the goals he wanted to achieve in addition to those specified in the brief.

One of his main concerns was for the patient's state of mind, a consideration given scant attention by engineers. Ockeloen refers to this bias as a "technocratic approach" in which the technology is the focus rather than patients and medical personnel.

The Integris C, as it was eventually named, is an X-ray stand used for interventional angiographic techniques, a procedure that is growing in its application (see Figure 7-13). Angiography permits the imagery of blood vessels. During an angiographic intervention, diagnosis as well as an attempt to remedy the malfunction are undertaken during the same procedure.

Figure 7-13. Visual form and user interface design contribute significant new value to complex medical equipment.

An X-ray system is used to generate a real-time image of the patient's blood vessels on a monitor with the aid of a catheter injecting a contrasting fluid. The catheter can be guided to the problem area, where both the diagnosis and treatment can proceed.

The stand is an essential part of the system, allowing the X-ray source and receptor to be perfectly in line at any projection. When a vascular stand is used it must be redirected to achieve various projections. Since this involves moving heavy parts that change position in relation to each other, the stable balancing of the system is a problem. Because this problem was thought to be unsolvable any other way in the past, heavy, noisy, and expensive motors were used to achieve balance. Other problems with equipment on the market in 1987 when PMS began development of its market entry in angiographic equipment were that the bulk and weight of the equipment provided poor patient access when an emergency, such as heart failure, requires getting the equipment out of the way as fast as possible. In addition, elements of equipment blocked a view of the patient and monitor when the operator stood at the control end of the stand.

Ockeloen worried about patients who are fully conscious during the procedure and who are undergoing an unpleasant intervention. They were being faced "with mechanical and optical devices spinning around him like he was a car body on a robotic assembly line," noted Ockeloen. He was also concerned about improving the performance level of the equipment in terms of mobility and improved visibility for the medical staff. User interface in existing equipment was primitive in its resolution.

Ockeloen, who gives top preference to designing medical products "because they offer this strange paradox of extremely advanced technology mixed with a rudimental design approach that make almost all these type of products look like engineering prototypes," advises that the best way to begin a design project for medical equipment is to spend a "lot of time hanging around hospitals" to find out about equipment, facilities, and how medical staffs work.

The Integris C, as conceived and ultimately designed by Ockeloen, solved bulk, mobility, and user interface problems by applying a fundamentally new approach to this kind of equipment. The choice, among several options, was for Integris C to be a ceiling suspended system to achieve maximum space and accessibility to the patient. In order to reduce the bulk and weight of the equipment, a new cast aluminum process producing a wall thickness maximum of only 5 mm enabled Ockeloen to conceive of a C-arc, C-arc joint, and ceiling arm.

As a result of this engineering breakthrough, to which Ockeloen gives a lot of credit, he had the freedom previously impossible in welded, thick-wall casting materials to develop the curved C-form concept. The C-arc and the articulated housings that capture cables, motors, bearings, and other parts dramatically improve the function and user interface requirements. The interacting elements of Integris C remain fully balanced in whatever projection it is positioned. Manual repositioning is done with ease, due to the reduced mass of the equipment.

These C forms also express a visual elegance in their repetition and extension of the imaginary circle from which the C is derived. A strong color accent is used to emphasize the C-arc shape while visually reducing its width and covering the large holes used to knock out casting cores. Other color accents on controls and switches soften the technology intimidation to the patient and, importantly, also serve as visual identification signals to medical staff.

Integris C was introduced at the end of 1989 at the RSNA (Radiologic Society of North America) and was enthusiastically received for its medical, technological, and industrial design qualities. It has received a number of design awards, including Best of Category of the 1990 ID Annual Review and the gold medal from Industrie Forum Hannover. Ockeloen sees the recognition of the design contribution to the Integris C as a benchmark in medical equipment in which the design of the product is the visual standard bearer for communicating engineering and technological advances.

The product's success is due to the close and positive teamwork over a two-year period among the designer, mechanical and electrical engineers, medical specialists, and commercial staff of PMS. In this project, as in all PMS development projects, management procedures were formalized. The team participants, which included all relevant disciplines, participated in the seven phases of the project from feasibility to production.

Ockeloen characterizes the development process as "little battles fought out between disciplines...which can be stimulating as long as all parties remain on speaking terms with each other and keep an absolute trust in the sincerity of each other. With the Integris C project these conflicts were solved in a professional way." He refers to points in the development when engineers needed to be persuaded that smaller motors could be used or that pure design solutions could be employed, such as plugging a giant socket into the C-arm to house a pack of cables rather than thicken the form of the C-arc to do the same job. These are the little battles that are the norm during development and in which designers should be free to participate and argue for their point of view on equal terms.

INTEGRIS C AND DESIGN MANAGEMENT ISSUES

The medical equipment industry, unsurprisingly, is conservative in product design matters. The technology matters very much, and there is a perception that design is largely a cosmetic application and of relatively small importance. This attitude overlooks the worthwhile contribution product designers can make to the user interface aspects of medical equipment. And, as Ockeloen points out, the patient's psychological and physical comfort is in need of an advocate.

At Philips a receptivity to at least listen to the case for design in the PMS group was implanted with the development of the harmonization program. As the initiator and leader of this program, which eventually everyone could accept as beneficial and pragmatic, CID had earned its stripes.

When I went to visit our PMS group in Santa Ana, California, to broach the subject of their design program, our status was at least sufficient to get their attention. The design situation at Santa Ana was one of those last straggling "unmanaged" loose ends I inherited. PMS/California hired its own design consultant for its products. I told the management that the design results were not as high-quality as CID designs for PMS/Eindhoven. When the division agreed to transfer the design function completely to CID, I handpicked a young Dutch designer, Antonio Atjak, to send to California. His work on the Platinum project, in which bulky, awkward-to-manipulate ultrasound equipment was radically reconfigured by mounting the monitor and controls on a floating, counterbalanced arm, persuaded the engineers to work with him to reduce the mass and significantly improve the user interface aspects of the equipment (see Figure 7-14). The Platinum set a new industry benchmark for the design of ultrasound equipment. Atjak gave *leadership to the development team effort.*

The Platinum project paved the way for strong design input to the Integris C. Both the design innovation of Platinum and the development process were widely publicized in trade publications and design media this recognition did not rain down entirely like pennies from heaven. The pump generally takes some priming. An investment in establishing credibility has to be patiently built.

I think an important design management function is to manage a public relations program for the design achievements of one's company. The intent is not to seek personal publicity but to make a legitimate statement about the contribution design makes to product success. This is important for several reasons. It enhances the design profession as a whole, by providing process information and making the case for the strategic importance of design to corporations. And

Figure 7-14. The Platinum proved the value of design to the Philips Medical Systems management.

increasingly, media publicity about product design is very good indeed for building a corporate identity among consumers, distributors, stockholders, and, in short, all the constituencies of a company. Finally, perhaps the most important constituency needing to be influenced about design is one's own company. There's nothing like positive media coverage *to build status within your company.* When others make the design case for you, your company associates take notice.

Submissions to design competitions, magazine annual design award programs (which are increasing at a healthy clip), and museum exhibitions—all these are tasks of design management. Cultivation of periodical writers about design and business matters is eminently worthwhile as good two-way avenues of information about design developments.

The outstanding design achievement of the Platinum merited, in my opinion, letting people who might be interested know about it. The amount of attention garnered by Platinum and the number of design awards it received make the PMS/Santa Ana group design believers. These accolades also did not go unnoticed in PMS/Eindhoven, setting up the environment for Ockeloen to make strong design input into the development of the Integris C. This product has also been warmly received as a design award winner and recognized by the medical equipment industry as a design innovation that enhances the technical and medical achievements of the equipment. Both of these products have set new benchmarks in the industry because of their design.

CASE STUDY:
VIDEOPHONE

The much-debated issue of the relative advantages of an in-house design staff versus use of external design consultants is at the center of this case study. The resolution of this matter had an unusual twist in which the "either/or" aspect of assigning the design commission was deftly sidestepped by a process that involved both in-house staff designers and consultants. The outcome was one that satisfied everyone's objectives, and, not incidentally, everyone's egos.

It happens from time to time, even in a company like Philips, which solidly supports its corporate design staff across most of the management spectrum, that a product group manager develops a yearning to bolt from the established product creation process to seek the services of a design consultant. There is nothing wrong with this if the reasons for doing it are valid, if the selection of the consultant is knowledgeable, and if the product creation process is managed within the design product creation team format. Satisfying the foregoing criteria, which will be discussed in more detail in this book's final section, very clearly involves design management. Unfortunately, "bolting" from the internally established design management process is often a true commando action. The product manager co-opts all the design management tasks, and the final results in every instance where this has happened at Philips has been a failed product in the marketplace.

The problem always begins with the first of the three criteria: the reasons for bringing in a design consultant. In this case study, the reason was typical. The product group, Philips Kommunikations Industrie AG (PKI), located in Nuremburg, Germany, is part of the Philips Communications Systems group. PKI has some of the responsibility for developing telephone equipment, including the new videophones being developed to benefit from the ISDN (Integrated System Digital Networks) technology, which were launched in Europe in 1992. A huge market for new telecommunications applications, including videophones, is expected to develop in the second half of the 1990s. The PKI product manager for videophones, in his enthusiasm for the market potential and in his desire to establish Philips at the forefront of a new technology, envisioned a product that would dazzle the trade and capture the interest of consumers. He believed he needed a "name" designer to accomplish this. The designer he selected, however, was not, in my opinion, the one to achieve these aims.

The CID design team manager for professional products, Johnny Lippinkhof, was deeply troubled by the development, for it was in his mind a rejection by the product manager of the capabilities of his design group. He was also disturbed that the role of CID in the product creation process was "going off the track." He came to inform me of the problem and suggested that a way to divert the ill-chosen consultant might be to suggest that the Philips Kommunikations Industrie AG (PKI) sponsor a design competition as a way to select a consultant designer. I vetoed that idea because it would be an unwieldy and inefficient approach to the problem and most likely fail in the objective of delivering a successful product.

My recommendation was to do two things. First, I would meet with the managing director of PKI and persuade him to stop the negotiations with the designer selected by his product manager. Second, I would propose an alternative approach. PKI would sponsor a workshop program to develop a number of concepts for the videophone. Both design consultants and CID would participate in the workshops, and the final design concept selection would be chosen by PKI management from among those submitted by the workshop participants. A final condition: I would select the consultant workshop participants.

This proposal was fully acceptable at the PKI senior management level and reluctantly agreed to by the product group management. I invited Frog Design Group of Germany and Fahnstrom and McCoy of the United States to join a CID team in the workshops, which were, in fact, a competition for the commission. The three groups represented three different design approaches. Frog would produce bold, exciting product concepts. Fahnstrom and McCoy would focus on human factors and consumer acceptance of a new technology. The CID team would understand the technology and how far to push the engineers toward adapting it for an accessible and appealing consumer product. The CID team would also be more attuned to the production requirements of the product.

The first workshop, which was held at PKI headquarters in Nuremburg, was a two-day briefing by the technical and marketing managers of PKI to present market research information and the state-of-the-technology-art.

Johnny Lippinkhof recalls that the first session was memorable for several reasons. It reconfirmed the value of involving design at these preliminary stages because in attempting to communicate the brief to the designers, the extent to which marketing and engineering issues were unresolved became immediately apparent. Designers began asking questions and making observations that had not occurred to the engineers and marketers. In fact, Lippinkhof notes that the workshop provided the first occasion for bilateral communications on this project between the technical and commercial people. The involvement of designers forced them to consider such basic and crucial issues as the size of the CODEC (the housing of the computer that transfers image to digital information) and whether it should be a desktop, floor, or wall-mounted element.

The workshop process was new to everyone except CID and Michael McCoy and Dale Fahnstrom, who had worked with CID before. Among the designers there was a certain reticence, since this was, after all, a competition. Professional pride was at stake. But as the work process progressed, information give and take overrode suspicions and uneasiness. Professional enthusiasm for problem solving showed itself to be the stronger reaction. During the second workshop the teams presented their concept models to the commissioners. The signature characteristics of each team were highly evident, giving the PKI management a rich and varied assortment of concepts from which to choose. (See Figure 7-15.)

Michael McCoy and Dale Fahnstrom concentrated on the premise that, although videophone has long been a promise of the future, in practice it could meet con-

Figure 7-15. Design consultants and Philips in-house design group collaborated in a "friendly competition" for concept development of the Philips launch of their videophone.

sumer resistance. The notion of being observed by a camera while conducting one of life's heretofore most mundane activities could be very off putting. The additional telecommunications options applied to a long-familiar task also presented possibilities for confusion and user resistance, in Fahnstrom and McCoy's opinion. They sought to neutralize these barriers by emphasizing user interface simplicity and bestowing a benign and even playful character to the design elements. A picture frame around the video screen was a friendly spoof of the high-tech specifications that accomplishes these communications feats.

The Frog team went completely in the other direction by emphasizing the exotica of a dramatic new technology. Their models presented exaggerated forms that were exciting and daring. Such designs would unquestionably announce that Philips was a presence in videophones.

The CID team opted for the strategy that would, after all the fireworks, present the producible product. The team's models focused on a design that would reflect in its appearance the achievement of a new, sophisticated technology but would also be sensitive to human interaction in its usability. The designs would be compatible with available technology and production capabilities.

In the end it was decided to continue the product design and development on a two-track approach by combining the best of CID and Fahnstrom and McCoy's ideas. The two teams collaborated to produce the final design for the videophone, which was executed by CID designer Thomas Overthun. A prototype was on display at the Geneva Telecommunications trade show in October 1991, and the final product was introduced in 1992.

Although the Frog team's concepts were not accepted, largely because they could not be produced, their involvement and the idea stimulation they injected contributed a great deal to the process. For their part, they say that the work approach was entirely new to them and was a process from which they also learned.

VIDEOPHONE AND DESIGN MANAGEMENT ISSUES

The proactive stance taken by CID to counter what we felt was a mistaken course of action by PKI was effective for many reasons. Most important of these was to produce the desired results for PKI. There were also other important outcomes of the redirection of the design of the videophone to a managed process rather than a hit-and-run product design delivered without full integration into the established product creation process.

The design workshop technique, which is now a well-established part of product creation with most product groups at Philips, was in this case new to the PKI group. They were discovering for the first time the benefits of *full and early integration of design into the product creation process.* One of the most important benefits is the expanded scope of thinking that designers can bring to the establishment of the brief itself. In the case of the videophone, this expanded scope not only improved technical and marketing planning for this market entry product but also extended the thinking to future generations of products and what they could technically provide, what the market would accept, when it would accept technological advances in the videophone, and how to plan for different market segments. All these questions were discussed in an environment benefiting from the questioning and experience diversification of designers who see things from different perspectives.

Although workshops are a way of design life at Philips, this one was unique in that the teams were working in competition with one another. Bringing in consultants to participate in workshops for the development of concepts had been done before at CID. When the lighting product division was seeking ideas from CID for adapting new technology to a lighting system for the office of the 1990s, four consultant designers were invited to join CID designers in a week-long workshop to develop concepts. In the case of the videophone, however, the commission award was not necessarily going to be awarded to CID. CID designers were on the same footing to compete for that award with the two other external consultant groups, with, if anything, a bias against CID as being too conservative in the minds of PKI to serve up the desired excitement for the new product.

The competitive element pushed everyone to perform. The CID team felt particularly pressured to prove itself when measured against the consulting teams. The team was anxious to establish confidence in its abilities with PKI and to bolster its own self-confidence in the face of the initial rejection by the videophone product manager. Members of the CID design team were pleased with the outcome and assert that the competitive aspect was positive by "lighting a fire under them" to deliver the best they could and for the learning experience in exchanging ideas and work approaches with consultant designers.

Thus, the workshop competition with its multiple benefits was a *design-led innovation in the product creation process.* In the crucial process of adapting a new technology to a marketable product, the design group found an acceptable way to steer the management of a technology innovation through the design and development phase. CID won the confidence of PKI to the extent that they assisted PKI at its request in the marketing phase by producing a series of videotapes about the design process. These tapes were distributed to sales personnel to build enthusiasm for the new videophone.

The videophone case study also demonstrates how *design management uses both corporate and external resources to good effect in achieving the goals of a product group.* One of the tasks of a senior design manager is to stay abreast of developments within the design profession and to maintain an international "intelligence file" of the qualifications and special capabilities of designers. An experienced design manager has more insight into making these evaluations about which design consultants are best suited for a specific task and can make better judgments than those not involved with the design process on a day-to-day basis. The designer initially selected by the PKI product manager was a respected designer, but he was not the best choice for this project. Jose Carreras is a famous opera star, but he is not the best choice for singing Wagnerian roles.

In fact, the emphasis on systems rather than one-off products in the 1990s is a strong contributor to the "anti-design-star" approach of this decade. Most products are part of product ranges or systems and are necessarily developed by teams working in close contact over long periods. The design hero of earlier decades is becoming an anachronism today. The final design for a product like the videophone is a composite of knowledge, creativity, and expertise contributed by a number of people.

CASE STUDY: ROTA '90 SHAVER SERIES

When a company enjoys dominance in market share, conventional wisdom says that conservatism characterizes strategic planning. Risks are held to a minimum, and caution prevails. Yet there are competitors out there, and clinging to the status quo has its own risks.

This is the situation describing the Philips highly successful shaver business. Philips has the largest sales volume of shavers in the world. Its unique rotary head technology has attracted millions of loyal users over the years. But the user profile has changed as a result of the preference for many young men for wet shaving. Regaining the interest of youths in electric shaving and establishing a lifelong habit of shaver use is a top priority for the Philips shaver business.

As Philips was planning its market launch in the late 1980s for a shaver series of the 1990s, the general market trend for global products such as the shaver had already become evident. The niche marketing era demanding product differentiation was in contradiction to rotary shaver production, which employs mass production with a high degree of automation to achieve the huge quantities needed for an economical global marketing program.

It was therefore understandable that the manufacturing engineers were hard-liners on design unification in order to preserve the economy-of-scale benefits that automation achieved. Product managers, however, recognized the marketing trend toward diversification and feared that ignoring it would also be costly. Requirements and trends were clear. The proper response was not. A design direction was necessary that would position flagship shaver series of the next decade in symmetry with both production economies and market diversification. The design philosophy and specification must also be persuasive enough to convince nervous production managers and marketers of its validity.

The design team, led by Englishman Frank Newman, began charting its strategy by selecting design criteria, which fell into two basic groups:

1. Criteria essential to the functional values of the product, such as handling by the user, ease of use, reliability, and convenience

2. Criteria allowing the consumer to personally identify with the product, such as color, materials, typography and graphic design, packaging, and promotion

A workshop was organized to draw in the fresh thinking and ideas of CID designers who work in other product areas. The concepts developed in the workshop resulted in a fundamental shift in the configuration and character of the Philips shaver. The 1980s shaver range, although technically excellent, was bulky, hard-edged, and generally more concerned with mechanical performance than comfortable use.

CID's growing assurance in applied ergonomics is nowhere more evident than in the final design for the ROTA '90 series (see Figure 7-16). The form and details pay meticulous attention to how the shape fits the hand, how the controls can be easily manipulated, the feel of the covering material skin. The performance of the shaver was also improved as a result of the closer, more comfortable shave made possible by the superb ergonomic application to the design.

The spirit of the design also reflects the experience and expressive vocabulary of lead designer Frank Newman, who previously designed portable audio equipment for Philips Singapore design center. His interest in design semantics as a result of that experience is evident in ROTA '90 designs.

The organic form of the proposed design was developed by Computer-Aided Design, without which a shape of such complexity would not be possible. The primary factor for achievability is the control throughout the entire design and development stages that CAD provides in translating the design to production. The closely integrated team of designers, mechanical and electrical engineers, toolmakers, and production engineers was able to refine the product into its

Figure 7-16. This flagship design for Philips shavers for the 1990s represents a significant contribution by the design team in addressing market segmentation.

final resolution with extensive use of CAD. The reduction of follow-up work that often occurs during the translation phase from CID models and model drawings to engineering and toolmakers' drawings was substantial.

Designers using CAD have to attain a high level of competence and understanding of the production process related to the product they are designing in order to be able to challenge the production process and equipment with respect to design concepts. That challenge cuts two ways: to push the potential of the production process to the limits for achieving design innovation and designing to the valid and realistic constraints of the production process. The more designers understand both of these outer and inner limits, the more they can contribute to the product creation process.

The critical issue of product differentiation was resolved by designing the series so that the basic shape and construction was common for all models. The electromechanical elements of the shaver are complex and sophisticated in their technology. All shavers, regardless of their visual presentation, must incorporate the same high-performance mechanism. This is the most cost-quality aspect of the production process. Differentiation was achieved by designing and constructing the basic form so that certain key parts are interchangeable. Design elements such as material finishes, graphics, color, storage cases, and pouches could express different images, such as "high-tech" or "classic" styles.

Flexibility in the model range was also achieved with such production techniques as in-mold foil technology, a new printing technique for the control panel. This technology was developed at the initiative of the designers. Laser marking and soft-touch surface finishes were other design applications that significantly contributed to both the high-tech image and differentiated specifications of the ROTA '90 shaver range. Because the ROTA '90 was designed with a modular approach and in close connection to the requirement of the scale and process of manufacturing, the more efficient mass production processes specified by the design such as laser marking and in-mold foil have been highly successful.

In its early market introduction stages, ROTA '90 exceeded sales targets in spite of the economic effects of recession in 1991. Market tests indicate the ROTA '90 is regarded as a significant improvement in both function and visual presentation in its form and finish throughout the entire range of models.

ROTA '90 AND
DESIGN MANAGEMENT ISSUES

The shrinking market for electric shavers is Philips' biggest worry. The necessity to hang on to its mature users of shavers while tempting young men to dry shaving is in seeming conflict with economy-of-scale tenets. But Computer-Aided Design techniques and the designer's capabilities to master this technology assistance provides the framework for dealing with the closely interlinked design and production process for this kind of product. The critical factor, however, is the creative ability to problem-solving that a designer brings to the technology.

The intense efforts of CID, spanning several years in the 1980s, to research CAD systems, install the system of choice, and concurrently organize a departmentwide CAD training program for the design department are without question paying off, not only in increased productivity and more efficient interaction with development and production engineers but also in the enormously expanded opportunities the computer offers designers to explore wide-ranging design solutions. Bringing this kind of critical resource to the product creation process is an example of the tasks involved with *managing design resources.*

A cluster of tools and techniques were bundled in resolving the design of a shaver program for the 1990s. In addition to the role of CAD, the shaver design group and those who participated in the concept development workshop drew upon their exposure to the new design philosophy of product semantics, which analyzes and translates into design expression the historic, social, or use context from which a product derives its emotional content. The product semantics philosophy was introduced to CID designers as part of my ongoing program to upgrade designer skills and maintain their currency with new design concepts and developments. Another philosophy, and, in fact, a new design discipline, is ergonomics. This specialized area of design concern receives a great deal of attention in CID, which will continue as systems become more interactive and complex and as the demand for individual products to be easier to use accelerates. Ergonomics was the dominant design focus in developing the ROTA '90 shaver series.

Design managers must keep their eyes on the far horizon, constantly scanning for trends and clues about the resources that will be needed for tomorrow's design creation. They need to know who the leading thinkers are in new areas inquiry. These are the people the design manager will bring in as consultants to work with staff designers or, in the case of companies without substantial design staff, to work directly with marketing, development, and production people. All these tasks related to developing the design capabilities of the company must be carried out on a day-in, day-out basis in anticipation of challenges such as those that faced the shaver design team.

The designer's ability to provide the means for product management to move from a policy of a global product with limited scope for variation to one of differentiation to appeal to different age groups and lifestyles depends on delivering product variations that do not compromise the critical efficiencies of mass production. In the case of ROTA '90, *the designer played a key role in setting the strategic direction for the shaver product group for the 1990s.* This will become even more obvious when succeeding product ranges, which build on the parent ROTA '90 group, are introduced. With the groundwork laid for lifestyle differentiation as a theme, new product ranges will be more clearly seeking market niches.

The *scope of design work* in the shaver product group clearly flows into the product planning activity. The leadership that the design team gave to product planning for the ROTA '90, in tackling the differentiation conundrum from the market analysis and product concept through to the all-important storage or transport case of the shaver, has further entrenched the design team in a closely integrated product management group process. The design team has proved its critical importance to the development process by carrying the banner of courage in setting a new strategic direction for the shaver business.

CASE STUDY:
THE PHILIPS COLLECTION

Several years before Philips' one hundredth anniversary in 1991, plans were stirring for celebrating the occasion. Given the independent behavior that is synonymous with the Philips culture, each business group was busy with ideas ranging from silly gadget gifts to ponderous books about the history of Philips. Rumors drifted about concerning large-scale exhibitions and gala events.

A committee was formed some four years in advance of the anniversary year. The committee, in typical bureaucratic fashion, aided and abetted unfettered expansion of centennial projects. No efforts were directed toward developing a theme or applying credible quality evaluations for approval of projects.

Judging that the quality aspects of the centennial had developed beyond control, I did feel I should make a case, at least, for the opportunity to focus the celebration on a useful business approach. No one had proposed in any meaningful way to develop and market new products specifically tied to the centennial.

I prepared a proposal for Jan Timmer, then senior director of consumer electronics, to consider the proposition that, since a company's products are the most important thing a company has to say about itself, Philips' 100 years of existence should be positioned to the public in terms of the design, technology, and functional excellence of its products. I proposed that a collection of products should be commissioned, spearheaded by consumer electronics and, following that lead, by the other product divisions. This collection would include advanced products for up-market consumers who are looking for the extra dimension reflecting their lifestyle, aspirations, and individuality. The Philips Collection would be a practical strategy for establishing a direct link among sophisticated, advanced design, integrated technology, brand image, and profitability.

Timmer was immediately supportive of my proposal. CID prepared concept brochures complete with imagery of product concepts that served as examples of the design and function I had in mind. The brochure described the Collection's purpose and proposed a broad plan for its implementation. The concept was approved by Jan Timmer in early 1990, and we were on our way to a 1991 launch deadline.

I appointed a task force within each product group in CID to be responsible for the Collection designs, and I was appointed chairman of the Collection steering committee. No products could be included in the Collection without my approval. In short, this was, in fact, as was well understood by the business groups, a program that was design driven and directed.

Throughout the span of the development of the Collection, Timmer gave it his vigorous and consistent support. Even during that most stressful period when he was suddenly catapulted to the presidency and with the pressures of dealing with Philips' financial and restructuring difficulties, Timmer declared himself available to me to give whatever support was needed to make the Collection a success. He had ordered nearly all other centennial events and projects terminated and closed the centennial office. The Collection became the flagship for marking the anniversary.

However, participation even across business group borders, let alone between product divisions in a corporate, cooperative product program, was new to Philips, and collaboration did not come easily. The consumer electronics audio group was the only one to put the full force of its support immediately and continuously behind the Collection. Other groups dragged their feet over various issues: rejection of the Collection color program; claims that the program interfered with long-range product plans; haggling about the program name; ambivalence about the concept of the program's duration, which had evolved into an ongoing program as a vehicle for introducing premium products each year; arguments involving codevelopment of marketing plans between the product divisions and national sales organizations. Product groups were continually joining and dropping out. The January 1991 launch target had to be postponed to June 1991 to compensate for time lost through indecision in the product development process. The ragged participation in this program, even with the full endorsement and expressed commitment of the president, is evidence that a top-down mandate may not be enough to drive a program.

By the end of 1990, however, participation by nine product groups was confirmed. Products designed specifically for the Collection were scheduled for production from January to late 1991. Design criteria and elements, which would serve to bind a multiyear effort in image building for the Collection, had been developed. Prototypes of the Collection range of products were presented to senior managers in the fall of 1990, and their positive reception to something they not only could see as individual products but also finally appreciate in their totality as a Collection eased the way for more responsiveness to marketing proposals. There was the beginning of acceptance for the idea that the permanence of the Collection program could provide a learning curve process for added-value marketing and merchandising strategies. See Figure 7-17 for examples of some Collection products.

The market launch took place beginning in the fall of 1991. An integrated program supported by CID-designed packaging, product graphics, product literature, and coordinated merchandising display and promotional materials for all Collection products was the centerpiece of visual coordination. Distribution outlets were selected from the highest-quality Philips' established retail outlets.

Individual national organization marketing plans were developed to focus on specific market characteristics, but coordination with the business groups was agreed in order to preserve the advantages and impact of the overall Collection coherency. The German national organization took early leadership in develop-

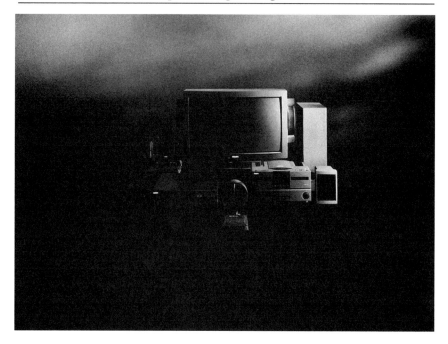

Figure 7-17. The close coordination of design, market strategy, and product launch of the Collection was carried out under the direction of design.

ing a creative and dramatic marketing program. Designed to capture the attention of target media, which included the quality shelter and design periodicals and news departments of mass media, openings launching the Collection were staged at prestige sites. One of these was the much publicized Vitra Design Museum in Weil am Rhein. The entire Collection was broadly presented in August 1991 at the Berlin Electronics Trade Show, which attracts an international audience. Openings were staged in Brussels, Amsterdam, Zurich, Malmo, Milan, and Paris in unique settings such as castles, a converted mill, and museums. The Beaubourg museum in Paris accepted the entire collection into its permanent collection of premier industrial design objects.

It is too soon to assess the long-term outcome of the Collection and the contribution it will make to establishing Philips firmly in the up-scale niche and building an image of a company with leadership in high-quality, innovative, and advanced-design products. It is also open to question whether the commitment to the program can be maintained over the long term. But the program was well conceived and timely both in terms of market movement toward added value as a dominant competitive success factor and for Philips itself, which was eager for a market success during a difficult economic period in order to attract favorable media attention that would focus on the strength of its design, technology strengths, and marketing resources.

THE PHILIPS COLLECTION AND DESIGN MANAGEMENT ISSUES

The program was conceived to meet *strategic corporate goals* of building the Philips brand image in the growing up-scale end of the market where consumer buying preferences are more demanding but yield higher profit margins.

This was a design-led program. It should continue to be under the general direction of design because the program's success depends on design criteria of aesthetic qualities that convey superior characteristics in both their form and technology.

The product launch required *managing corporate resources* to shape the program to meet strategic goals. I appointed my most creative designers to the product design task force; created an ad hoc project coordinator position, which was assigned to one of CID's seasoned designers, Fons Labohm; and personally hand-held the program in order to exert influence on the quality and direction of marketing plans and execution.

The design director is ideally suited to carry out this cross-the-business-group function. I was able to keep the goals, which, in the final analysis, have to do with quality, clearly on target because I have no particular vested interest in any single business group. My goal is to act as a *force for quality,* which underpins all activities from design to market. Quality results of stipulated goals will almost inevitably lead to the achievement of the goal for every company: profitability.

In spite of the various problems in prodding the business groups into a cohesive effort, the premise that design is a key factor for success in appealing to the added-value demands of ever-growing groups of consumers was never challenged. The crux of the problem was in the commitment demanded from development budgets and, even more thorny, from advertising and promotional budgets. Business groups were essentially being asked to make budget commitments over which they would not have full autonomy, since the program's overall direction took a certain number of product and marketing decisions out of their hands.

However, of all the centennial projects, many of which deserved their early death, the fact that this program survived demonstrates that design can have a powerful influence on directing a company toward keeping its eye on achieving strategically important goals and can stand as an uncompromising force for quality.

CASE STUDY:
THE EVOLUON

The design process has been described as messy. Emotional and sometimes irrational reactions can erupt from people who are normally very rational, competent, and cool-headed. I have observed that this is especially true when the design project is involved with corporate buildings and interior design. Apparently there is a truth here about pride of ownership and a personal imprimatur that carries over from one's home to the home-away-from-home—the place where one works. The Philips Evoluon project illustrates the kind of facilities design project that stirs complex and deeply felt emotions.

The Evoluon was a science and technology museum which was conceived and operated by Philips. It had been commissioned by then-president Frits Philips as a celebration memorial of Philips' seventy-fifth anniversary. When it opened in 1966 it was a sensation, drawing visitors from all over Europe to Eindhoven, the home base of Philips, to look in amazement at exhibits describing science and technology achievements. The architecture of the Evoluon was in itself a metaphor for the future with its spaceship/flying saucer configuration.

The Evoluon became a Philips icon. There was justified pride in what it signified: a company on the leading edge of scientific and technological innovation. (See Figure 7-18.)

By the time I took up my duties at Philips in 1980, what I saw during the number of visits I made to the Evoluon to study its exhibitions and observe what was going on was that it had become worn-weary from 15 years of heavy traffic. The Evoluon had also not borne its futuristic architectural metaphor well. Like its dated flying saucer imagery, the exhibitions suffered from poor maintenance and old information. In short, the Evoluon had not kept up with the changing times.

Like a cherished family possession that has lost its luster, the tarnish was obvious to outsiders but not to the family—Philips executives failed to see that the Evoluon was not what it once was. They had not even observed that traffic

Figure 7-18. A company icon that had outlived its purpose was redesigned to become "the front door of Philips"—an information and meeting center for the varieties of publics with whom Philips has a relationship. (*Photographs by Burdick Group*)

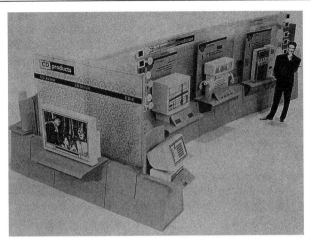

Figure 7-18. (Continued)

was falling, that it had become a recreational romp for school children on rainy days while teachers chatted over coffee in the cafeteria.

My interest in exhibitions goes back to my association with Charles Eames, who set a standard for presenting complex information in fascinating and understandable ways with exhibits such as those he designed for IBM and the U.S. government. Designers who worked in his office, including Bruce Burdick, Robert Staples, and Barbara Charles, continued to develop the art of exhibition design in their own design offices and helped keep me in touch with state-of-the-art techniques for presenting information.

I was dismayed at what I saw at the Evoluon and expressed this reaction to Board of Management member Arthur van Mourik. He listened and reported my opinions to Philips president, Wisse Dekker. Dr. Dekker, as a result, exerted pressure to see that, at a minimum, the exhibits were operating. But a fundamental upgrading of the facility and exhibitions was an idea that languished for several years.

During the presidential tenure of Cor van der Klugt, an evaluation was made of the sprawling inventory of buildings not directly related to business functions that Philips owned and operated. The costs of maintaining this real estate empire ran counter to the companywide cost cutting and restructuring that was being undertaken. A Philips committee, which had conducted the study, recommended that instead of spending money and effort to upgrade these facilities, exhibition sites which were sprawled all over Holland at various product division locations and meeting places should be consolidated to a single facility. The Evoluon was the candidate for this centralized information and meeting center.

There was widespread resistance to any change to the Evoluon. The resistance seemed to be connected with sentiment for "the good old days" when Philips commanded a multinational empire and the Evoluon expressed its achievements. But the Dutch are also hard-headed realists. The costs of supporting superfluous, outdated real estate, in some quarters, took priority over sentiment. A vision of what the Evoluon as an information center should be was less clear.

I was a member of a series of evolving committees over a period of several years whose task was to deal with these facility problems. When the problem of an outdated Evoluon, badly in need of both a physical refurbishing and a new purpose, collided with the facility inventory problem in general, the committee began to seriously consider a fundamentally new role for the Evoluon. But what should be housed in the Evoluon/Information Center? What should be done about "the flying saucer" architecture? Who would do the design work? Who would pay for it?

The committee asked my advice about a design approach for the interiors and exhibitions. Although I suggested a design competition for selecting the exhibition designer, the committee chose to shortcut the process and asked me to make a selection. I selected the Burdick Group, based on their experience and their voluntarily submitted proposals for how the building could be used and concepts for exhibitions. Bruce Burdick and Susan Burdick proceeded to do a formal proposal.

The Burdick proposal accepted the idiosyncratic character of the Evoluon architecture, emphasizing its circular form rather than trying to camouflage it. The exhibitions were to be designed to lead the visitor in a continuous circular direction through three "rings" or floors of exhibitions, each with its own communication responsibility to present the core competencies of the company in the context of the process of technology research and subsequent application to new products. Much of these stories would be communicated by the very interactive audio and video products that are themselves the subjects of the information presentations.

The reception of the Burdick conceptual proposal was, in principle, positive. However, what later caught us by surprise was a combination of misperception of the concept and outright resistance from the product divisions when it came to a commitment of support with resources and participation.

The Burdick proposal instituted the concept that the Evoluon would combine both meeting places and exhibition needs in one central location—the Evoluon. As Bruce Burdick described it, the Evoluon, which would add the phrase *Competence Center* to its name, would be the "front door" to Philips—a focus point that the company previously lacked. "As a visitor or employee, it was always hard to gain an understanding of the company as a whole. In the future Philips will be able to express itself as a company through the Competence Center."

The proposal for the Evoluon included concepts for a new structural addition to house an auditorium and to retrofit an existing adjacent building for a dining room, VIP lounges, meeting rooms, and offices. It was decided that the Philips Architecture and Engineering Bureau would undertake the architecture task. The Burdicks recommended cleaning up the interior of the Evoluon itself, stripping it of interior architectural clutter and allowing the unique nature of the architecture to assert itself.

The misperception of the concept became evident when I discovered that the Evoluon committee during my absence of several meetings due to business travel had taken some off-the-track actions. Some committee members had failed to grasp the difference between a commercial exhibit of products, such as that of a trade show, and the larger, instructional overview concept intended for the Competence Center.

The committee in my absence had hired a local trade show exhibit design firm to develop concepts for the Evoluon exhibits. This firm went beyond its assignment and recommended an expanded array of Disneyesque buildings to house additional bell-and-whistle exhibits and other related activities. These ideas had all the trappings of the commercialism and short-term focus of trade show exhibits plus an additional attempt to impose a veneer suggestive of entertainment to the whole project. Some of the committee members were very enthusiastic about the proposal of the local exhibit design firm, indicating that they hadn't understood the basic premise of the Burdick concept. Their enthusiasm also reflected the penchant for embracing what one is familiar with rather than risking a new idea.

The product division managers, in response to this proposal, declared, "Who needs it?" They pointed out that they already had display rooms at their respective headquarters where they showed their range of TVs, audio equipment, telephone equipment, and so on. They rejected, with justification, the idea that they should spend money for the kind of exhibit that the local exhibit designers were proposing. But without understanding the Burdick proposal, largely because the waters had been muddied with the second intervening proposal, the baby was being thrown out with the bath water. They rejected in total doing anything.

For my part, I saw that the design control had been diffused and the resulting confusion jeopardized the whole project. Jan Timmer, who was by now president, took a strong personal interest in the Evoluon. When he asked me for a progress report, I briefed him on the problems of lack of support of the product divisions and how that had happened. He requested that the Burdicks make a personal presentation to him of their proposal. In that meeting, which I attended, Timmer endorsed the Burdick proposal and told me he would make clear to everyone involved that I had full authority to direct the Evoluon design activity. This responsibility included approving and coordinating the work of the architects with that of the Burdicks.

The painstaking work of educating the product division management to the concepts of the Burdick proposal began. Personal presentations were made over a period of months, with updated meetings to explain the Burdicks' exhibition ideas as their work progressed. This process, especially in the beginning, was as much about changing the stereotype in thinking about "exhibits" as it was to gain support for the details of the information and the way it would be presented.

Because meeting space was badly needed as a result of the closure of other facilities, the architectural and interior retrofitting work was given priority for completion so that the building could be used. It seemed appropriate to officially open the "new" Evoluon during the Philips one hundredth anniversary year in

1991. With festive fanfare, this was accomplished in September 1991 with Queen Beatrix attending the event.

The exhibition, which will include a Philips history section, and the "ring" displays of Philips global competencies in research, design, manufacturing, marketing, and human resources as they are applicable to the various product divisions, will open in 1993.

THE EVOLUON AND DESIGN MANAGEMENT ISSUES

This project marked the first time that as director of Corporate Industrial Design I was given full design authority for a nonproduct design project. This was a significant breakthrough in recognizing the role of design in developing a corporate identity. Indeed, the crux of the problems that arose in the Evoluon project can be attributed to misconceptions about what corporate identity really is. The absence of design input except at the incidental soliciting of advice from time to time by scattered managers, and the fragmentation of what would normally be considered corporate identity tasks across product divisions and national organizations, meant that Philips really did not engage in a consciously conducted corporate identity program. For that reason, there was a widespread failure to make the connection between how Philips was presenting itself to its various publics in the "old" Evoluon and the negative impact it was causing for Philips. In the process of creating a new use for the Evoluon, marketing people approached the problem as if it were a commercial product launch rather than seeing it as a long-term corporate identity presentation of Philips in the totality of its competencies and core businesses.

These misperceptions of the nature of corporate identity overlooked the valuable use that could be made of the Evoluon to present the face of Philips to its employees, customers, stockholders, the media, government officials, and other influential opinion makers. Misperceptions also contributed to the emotional reluctance to reposition a company icon, the resistance of product divisions to finance the costs of something they considered unnecessary (because they misunderstood the purpose of the Burdick proposal and how it would be carried out), and the confusion that grew out of a number of people working at cross-purposes.

When the project was stabilized with clear management authority delegated to the design director by the president, the damage caused by emotions, resistance, and confusion was able to be repaired. The most important repair work was that of convincing the product divisions that the Evoluon could make an important contribution to *the strategic goals of Philips* by presenting an image to its publics that had not previously been successfully communicated.

Thus, design management brought order out of confusion. Because of the successful resolution of this project, an opportunity had been created to educate a broad spectrum of Philips people to the process of conceiving and managing an element of a corporate identity program.

The results in terms of the building redesign and the excellence of the exhibitions in their concept and execution are now a permanent example of how Philips can present itself in a coherent and qualitative way to all the people who have a relationship with the company. Because the *project was design-driven,* the future involvement of design in helping to craft a true corporate identity program for Philips is now understood by many people to be both logical and advantageous.

The longer-range benefit from the Evoluon in terms of a *strategic contribution to Philips is that it paved the way for developing a true corporate identity program.* Jan Timmer created a corporate identity portfolio at the board level and, further, added this subject as a task force assignment for the Philips Centurion—the restructuring and strategic planning group composed of the top 100 senior managers. The task force was organized at the end of 1991 under the chair of Dr. Thierry Meyer, member of the Board of Management, and included representatives from product divisions, national organizations, corporate communications, public relations, external affairs, and corporate industrial design. I served as external consultant. The task force assignment was to recommend an action plan to improve Philips brand and corporate image through corporate identity and communication policies. The scope for action included:

- Corporate identity and house style
- Product design and packaging
- Marketing communications
- Exhibitions
- External communications
- Internal communications

Philips had crossed the threshold from being a company with widely diffused elements of corporate identity spread across its vast organization to recognizing that the need to present itself more effectively through a structured and well-planned corporate identity program.

PART FOUR

A BASIS FOR BUILDING A DESIGN MANAGEMENT METHODOLOGY

Design Management and Some Common Ground for All Companies

The case study descriptions of design activities and how they were managed at Herman Miller and Philips in these two very different but design-committed companies suggest that there is some common ground for design managers and their role no matter what the size of the company is, where it is located, or what business it is in. The common ground for design managers can be summarized this way:

1. The early and continuous involvement of design across the scope of activities from design research to market launch is a key to product success. A structured design management process must be functioning effectively to drive the design contribution through the stream of activities related to the product creation process.

2. Networking for establishing or improving the working relationships of cross-functional teams, in which the designer can make a significant contribution, and, in some cases, provide leadership, is a critical task for all design managers.

3. The emphasis or focus of the design management mission will be different for each company depending on the degree of commitment to design as an integrated element in its strategic operations. In general, the larger and more complex the company, the greater the need to continually reinforce the commitment to design.

In the early days of Herman Miller, when it was a small company, ensuring that the small management family "kept the design faith" was a simple matter. When the company burst into expansion in the mid-1970s, it was much like any other company in the uneven degree to which individual managers in marketing, engineering, and production truly understood the role of design.

At Philips in 1980, although design was well-established and accepted as a function of product creation, the design management mission was to convince everyone that the level of design quality needed to be raised. Support had to be mustered to obtain the resources and change the process to achieve that quality improvement.

4. The tasks of design management are essentially common to all companies: to marshall and manage the resources needed to make certain design can deliver what it promises.

5. Communication about design to the entire company is the most essential task of the design manager in accomplishing the design mission and managing the design process. The true creativity in design management is in the communication effort. It develops, nurtures, and tills what I and my group of designers (both on staff and consultants) at Herman Miller called the "fertile ground for design."

That communication is at two levels: the constant buzz level, about which more will be said in the next chapter, and at the situation target level. At Herman Miller, for example, both Charles Eames and the president, Hugh De Pree, needed to be persuaded that the Tandem Seating for O'Hare Airport was a worthwhile financial risk for Herman Miller and a worthwhile time investment in design for Eames. Though others in the management group were unconvinced, the two people that mattered were persuadable. At Philips, the crucial harmonization program, which was the framework for improving the quality level of design as a whole, had to have a godfather. I persuaded Vice President Gerrit Jeelof to be the godfather, thus paving the way for persuasion of the senior managers of the professional products groups. In time, the harmonization program was accepted at all operational levels and spread to other product divisions. President Jan Timmer was the champion of the Collection and Evoluon projects. Locating crucial pressure points of influence, communicating the problem, and gaining support for the cause is the quintessential design management task.

STRUCTURE MATTERS

Although earlier chapters have referred to the organizational structure of design, some points need to be elaborated. The design activities described in the previous chapters took place during a specific slice of time—at Herman Miller from 1960 to 1979 and at Philips from 1980 to 1991. During these respective periods the design programs at both companies underwent significant changes in their overall structure and in how the design process was carried out.

Herman Miller's design program evolved during the period from being consultant-directed to being managed in-house. As vice president for design my task was to orchestrate the activities of both Herman Miller's own design staff and those of outside consultants. The design function at Philips was under centralized management during the early years of my tenure in order to bring activities under greater control, thereby achieving dramatic improvement in the design quality of Philips products. The structure and process were also altered during that period in a continuous direction of devolving responsibility downward and horizontally throughout the design organization.

In both cases, the design organization reflected the signal changes gripping the companies. Herman Miller grew from a company that produced low-volume, prestigious residential furniture to a mass-volume producer of furniture systems for the office and institutional market. Philips experienced a massive restructuring in order to shift from a duplicative function multinational corporation to one that became product-directed on a global basis. The conclusion from studying these two companies is that the dynamics of change in corporations, as they struggle to keep pace with the changes in the business environment, demand that the structure and process of design must also be fluid. It is a key task of the design manager to anticipate and act on these company changes in the way he or she organizes and carries out the design function. Anticipation is a critical factor. By taking proactive measures, the design manager can create the most advantageous change rather than allowing the design operating status to be dictated by staff bureaucrats or other functional managers. The three-zone strategy I planned for the Philips design organization was well in advance of the actual structural changes that occurred at Philips but synchronized precisely when they did take place.

One thing is certain for the foreseeable future. Corporations will be constantly searching for the appropriate structural format for competing in the global economy, and design managers will have to be agile in detecting new directions and acting on shifts in corporate structuring and policies. No one has the golden answer, especially for achieving the ideal balance between centralization and decentralization. The almost zealous embracing of decentralization by companies in recent years has created a whole new set of problems, especially for managing design. The relatively few companies that have forged a strong design program have been able to do so in previous decades on the basis of a centralized "command post" for achieving a design program coherency. Decentralization poses problems and threats to maintaining that coherency. Ironically, a strong and consistent corporate image is even more crucial for a company with decentralized operations. Its products and communications are *the* unifying elements in regional and global markets. But the demands and character of decentralized operations pull design management of products and communications in two directions. This design issue of managing a global design organization will present a formidable challenge for design management in coming years.

GETTING THE ORDER OF THINGS RIGHT

In the Philips overview section, I described a step-by-step process for achieving the goal to improve the quality of product design. Briefly, these steps were first to strengthen the centralized design organization in its structure, process, and resources. A beginning was then made to tame the design chaos resulting from independent actions in numerous design groups around the world. The harmonization program was the centerpiece for providing design guidance and coherency. Other programs and resources were added, which were described or referred to in the case studies.

The reader may recall that the reality of decentralization (the three-zone policy) was always riding copilot with these actions to bolster design quality. But we needed to have a well-established, strong central design program to ensure the success of the decentralized activities. My belief that a strong central design program must be maintained is based on the following rationale:

1. Some staff functions cannot, or at least should not, be duplicated in regional design centers or groups. As the design process becomes more complex, requiring a bundling of state-of-the-art skills such as ergonomics, information design, user interface design, as well as product graphics and packaging design, it is unrealistic, even for a company with a design staff the size of Philips', to provide these necessary skills at every design location. They are a central resource.

Complete and up-to-date tools such as CAD are more likely to be researched in a central location. Training for using these tools is also an essential activity best carried out at one central location. Materials research and other design information resources need to be centralized, although designers at regional centers can make an important contribution to that research by carrying out task assignments that enrich the central information resource center. Communicating this centralized information to satellite design locations should be increasingly efficient with the variety of telecommunications media available now.

2. Networking with other corporate staff functions at corporate headquarters is a practical necessity. Personnel activities, financial planning, and budgetary interaction need to be coordinated with peer staff managers in these functional areas.

3. Recruiting, hiring, and training staff designers has to be carried out on the basis of the goals and needs of the entire design organization as well as those of the commissioners. A program of skill and knowledge upgrading must be centrally planned and implemented. Design consultant selection should also be consistent with the strategic plans of the company and compatible with design policies and aesthetic profile of the company's product or communications design. These activities are also a central design management task.

4. Design coherency and quality can only be achieved from the impetus of leadership. That leadership has to be rooted in the firm foundation of design policy and connected to the strategic planning of the company.

SENDING DESIGNERS OUT FROM THE CENTER

The case for decentralized design groups is a potent one, and for all the same reasons that the corporation decentralizes: to be close to its markets and to achieve production efficiencies. To be part of the development team, designers must be "on location" in key production centers.

Our experience at Philips CID with the decentralization process has been most successful when product division managers have fully understood and supported the role of the central design organization.

We have basically operated on two levels of decentralization. Groups of five to ten product and product graphic designers are located in international production centers (IPCs) which design, develop, and produce products for Philips worldwide. We call these centers of competence. These design groups are headed by strong, experienced designers selected from the CID designer pool. They participate in the product planning activities to a considerable extent in their "outpost" location and exercise a great deal of freedom of judgment and decision making in the product creation process. However, these designers are guided by CID design policies, and harmonization programs and maintain regular communication and consultation with CID Eindhoven. They retain their full association as CID personnel and are assured that their career development will be managed by CID.

At the second level of decentralization designers are located at production sites which are primarily just that: factories for production. In this case product planning and design is done at product division headquarters and at CID/Eindhoven. The designer's task is limited to design quality control and interacting with manufacturing.

An example of an upper-tier decentralized design group and how it functions is the Singapore group. Singapore is a center of competence and IPC for personal audio and video products—radios of all kinds and other portable music equipment. The CID Singapore expatriates are closely involved in product planning and serve as an important design research resource to the Singapore product management team. The designers source suppliers and work with the development team in spin-off factories in Malaysia as well. Because audio and video products are increasingly being designed as parts of product systems, the Singapore designers have frequent communications with their CID colleagues in Eindhoven, Hong Kong, Tokyo, and Vienna, where centers of competence and IPCs are located for other audio and video products. At least twice a year, the Singapore designers meet at one of these locations with their CID colleagues for a workshop session, during which the designers collaborate to develop program design concepts. Trade shows and regional design conferences also provide contact with CID associates, as do the periodic visits to Singapore by CID senior management.

The key to the success of the decentralized design program is the experience of the on-location design manager, who is well grounded in CID policies and process, frequent personal contact with CID colleagues and managers, and a regular two-way flow of communications.

The issue of centralized versus decentralized design operations generally seems to come down on the side of a strong link from the central design office to satellite groups. Japanese companies for the most part are strongly centralized. Sony, Yamaha, and Canon are all centrally design directed. Sharp has nearly a third of its designers at its central headquarters with the other designers distributed around Japan at product division headquarters. But the direction by design director Kiyoshi Sakashita is firmly in hand. He rotates his designers between divisions and headquarters, maintaining coherence with the total design organization.

The greatest danger of design decentralization is disconnection. Without a strong bond to a central design unit, designers, singly or in small groups, will inevitably become the servant of marketing or manufacturing, carrying out product designs to the specifications of others. Disconnected from resources for creative stimulation, professional growth, and access to information about new design techniques and tools, the talented designer will become bored, burned out. The routine-comfortable designer will plod along and will produce routine designs. The disconnected design group becomes a liability to the corporation. Indifferent designs, lacking visual cohesion with the total corporate image, weaken the product and communications projection of the corporation.

In these circumstances, perhaps an alert product manager will notice that, as a result of an isolated and uninfluential design group, the product designs are not up to the mark. The product manager will decide the solution is to hire a design consultant. With no credentials for researching and making a decision about the choice, the product manager will hire a consultant. The design direction to the consultant is in the hands of the non-design-experienced product manager or perhaps the development engineers. The staff designers are further demoralized, and the design results are most likely to be even more out of synchronization with the corporate identity. An important design management task, therefore, is close communication and overview direction from the centralized design organization in order to "keep connected" and maintain coherent design quality.

HOW TO CHOOSE: IN-HOUSE DESIGN STAFF OR CONSULTANTS?

The disconnected, decentralized divisions or business units, dangling on their own without a centrally managed design program, further muddy an already unclear picture about the relative advantages of using design consultants or relying on an in-house design staff. There are no credible, hard-and-fast guidelines for making this decision. Look around at companies who seem to be doing a decent job of product and communications design and you'll see a polyglot approach to the issue.

Having been design director in both situations, one involving a strong reliance on external consultants (Herman Miller) and the other functioning with a large and competent in-house design staff (Philips), I think the choice was right for each of those companies. The experience with both approaches also convinces me that there are advantages and disadvantages to each, and that only an intimate understanding of a company's unique culture, what it does and how it does it, can point the direction to how the design activity should be carried out. The one general rule to observe in either case is that there should be a strong design management capability to direct either the internal design staff or to recruit and manage external consultants.

The arguments for either choice on their own merits are fairly obvious, a company's particular culture, strategies, work processes, and so on notwithstanding.

An in-house staff lives and breathes the daily life of the company and therefore is in a position to project the corporate identity in products and communications more authentically and appropriately. Even more important, the product creation process is now understood to be at its most effective if it is conducted with a tightly knit multidisciplinary team of which the designer is the core. The necessarily close day-to-day interaction of the team raises questions about the practical inclusion of external consultants.

However, on the other hand, designers on staff in small companies or companies with narrow product lines are understandably subject to boredom, churning out, as a result, stale, uninspired work. Mediocre designers will be content with such a routine; good, ambitious designers will not. The result, the argument goes, is that designers on company staff tend to be less talented than those in their own practice who thrive on the diversity of clients and tasks. However, the trend in increase in the size and number of company design staffs in recent years and the impressive quality of work coming from in-house staffs would tend to refute this standardized assumption. No one would suggest that Japanese competitors across the spectrum of industries with their large design staffs are turning out inferior design work.

A sample of companies across a range of industries of industries offers no conclusive evidence that one choice is superior to the other. Dictaphone has been building its in-house design staff under the direction of Sandor Weisz in order to regain lost market share. Product design improvement is central to the company's mission to transform its image. Digital Equipment's in-house design staff is finally breaking the barrier between product designers and engineers, winning respect for their contribution to team effort, and "formalizing" their participation in the product creation process. Olivetti, however, has relied for years on the talents of consultant designers such as Ettore Sottsass Jr., Hans von Klier, Mario Bellini, and, more recently, Michele De Lucchi. Olivetti is considered a design leader in computers, and obviously the company culture is such that even in a highly technical product, designers are able to have a good relationship with engineering designers. Erco Lighting Company, a prestigious design leader in contemporary lighting systems, also stakes its reputation on the work of consultant designers such as Emilio Ambasz and Roy Fleetwood. But the German company's CEO, Klaus-Jurgen Maack, closely supervises all external consultants for design and communications, including product designers, graphic designers, and copywriters. Acting as his company's design director,

Maack leaves nothing to chance, since he believes mediocre design would threaten his total corporate strategy.

Some kind of combination of in-house staff and consultants is undoubtedly the ideal solution. The mix and the way in which staff and consultants are used is a matter for sensitive judgment and continuous fine-tuning. It is one of the most important tasks of design management to make and orchestrate these decisions.

Sometimes what may seem to be logically workable isn't for reasons specific to the company. At Herman Miller, with its deeply rooted and successful tradition of relationships with design consultants, the decision was made at a point in its growth and shift in emphasis from low-volume residential and executive office furniture to high-volume institutional and commercial systems to expand the in-house design staff. The reasons seemed logical. A great deal of design work was necessary to adapt basic products to specific user requirements. The consultants were uninterested in these mundane but critical design problems. And indeed, having made the commitment to the office and institutional market, it was not guaranteed that George Nelson or Charles Eames, in particular, would respond to the design task of feeding the supply line with new product/system designs.

But the in-house design staff I assembled really never developed beyond the competency for extending the concepts of Eames, Nelson, and Propst. Although the principle of growing our own designers was accepted, it was not supported with sufficient resources to adequately recruit and support good talent. This was most certainly a matter of attitude. The internal staff designers, who were certainly competent, never bridged the differences in respect that outside consultants were accorded. Eventually the product design staff idea withered and faded away.

It's Not Necessarily a Case of Either/Or

The culture for a strong in-house design staff was well established when I joined Philips. It became clear to me that the intricate relationships of designers with development and marketing people in the product divisions justified the large internal design staff, but it was also clear that an infusion of new thinking and guidance in upgrading skills was needed. The Philips case studies refer to the variety of ways consultants have been brought in to accomplish these objectives. They have conducted workshops to introduce new design philosophies, such as semantics and user interface. They have collaborated with CID designers in workshops devoted to developing concepts for new products, and consultants have had a relationship over a period to introduce new skills to our designers. John Rheinfrank of Fitch, Richardson, Smith and Bill Moggridge and his colleagues at IDEO have participated in user interface seminars to accelerate the learning curve of the 15 CID designers who have specialized skills related to this area of expertise.

Although using consultants in these ways is well accepted (and usually paid for by product division commissioners) and for the most part welcomed with enthusiasm by CID designers, it is a matter to be handled with delicacy. In the view of Philips designers, consultants who are brought in to provide information and skill upgrading or to collaborate on concept development is a far different matter from engaging a consultant to parachute in to do a product design. Staff designers become demoralized. They question the durability of the relationship they have built with commissioners. Self-confidence wavers. Generally, on the few occasions when this has happened at Philips as a result of a product manager's commando action, the product manager has defended the hiring of a consultant by explaining that the product would benefit from having a "star" designer's name attached to the product. This confuses public relations with the goal to design products consistent with the family range of Philips products. In any case, I doubt that most of the customers for consumer, professional, or industrial products have any awareness of designer names. Few product designers are in the celebrity mainstream.

From the other side of the story, architect-designer Emilio Ambasz comments that in his experience as consultant he encounters barely concealed resentment from staff designers, who, he says, are often invisible in their influence with the corporation. Their hostility to the consultant is acted out by doing as little as possible to facilitate the follow-up detail work with engineers and production people. Ambasz sympathizes with their ego problems, blaming the low status of staff designers for the strained relationship. A design management gap clearly exists in this kind of situation, which is probably more usual than not. There are certainly ways to motivate the staff in day-to-day responsibilities so that they have the confidence in themselves and consequently have a better relationship with a consultant. For example, at Philips I instituted a Director's Award for internal designers, building it into a ceremonial event. And each year we publish and display the "Best of CID," which are peer-selected awards chosen from the body of design work for that year. The designers regard this as an important recognition of their work. Product groups have picked up on the idea, and some now sponsor their own best design-of-the-year event. Giving in-house designers credit in external media and award programs is also important.

Sharp's design director, Kiyoshi Sakashita, sponsored a "New Technology Art" exhibition, which was displayed in the Axis building in Tokyo. It is an interesting project in that it is an in-house competition among his 200-plus design staff. His purpose was to encourage the designers to unshackle themselves from the normal constraints of business and create totally uninhibited designs. The theme for the competition selected by Sakashita, however, was related to a field that Sharp is investing in—future technology development. The concept of the competition is excellent, since it is an exercise in creativity apart from the daily tasks of design and it gives public recognition to the best of Sharp's designers.

A related problem for consultants and their clients is that the consultant may be dealing with the wrong person—often at too low a level in the company—to effectively accomplish what both the client and consultant hope for. Bruce Burdick, product and exhibition designer, quips that when he has been contracted to design an exhibition and he is told to report to the company facilities manager he knows he's got problems. The client expects a first-rate exhibit to communicate something important but handicaps the consultant designer by coupling her or him with someone of both narrow responsibility and understanding of the nature of the project. This is another example of a design management gap.

Regardless of the size of the in-house staff or the proportional mix between staff and consultant project assignments, there are relationships to manage and work to facilitate. Even if there is no design staff at all, someone needs to manage the relationship and work process between the consultant and the appropriate persons he or she works with in the company.

Aside from the familiar consultant task assignment to design a product or communications project, consultants can support and augment even the most sophisticated in-house staffs in a number of important ways. Two of these have already been described as consultant activities at Philips:

- Providing new skills and information

- Participating in concept development with design staff when supplemental expertise in a particular area is needed

There are other consultant contributions that companies who want to be serious about their design capabilities should consider:

- Providing an assessment of the skill level and competency of the internal design staff

- Acting as auditors for the body of corporate design work output, including product and communications and environment design

Just a few months after I joined Philips I invited Niels Diffrient, an acknowledged authority on human factors design, to come to Eindhoven to familiarize himself with our design group and to help me assess what needed to be done to boost our capabilities in this crucial aspect of design. His evaluations and recommendations put the Philips design group on the path to our present level of capability in user interface design.

The rapidly developing area of user interface design has focused attention on ergonomics, user interface, and on-screen information design, all of which demand specialized skills. The CID designers who work together in teams with product and graphic designers will need intensive and continuing exposure to new technology developments and the design skills to respond to these. The design director should be constantly scouting for the most knowledgeable people who can evaluate the competency level of the designers and make remedial recommendations.

INFUSING A LITTLE OUTSIDE OBJECTIVITY

An external audit team for the evaluation of the total corporate image is an idea whose time has clearly come. Harvard professor Robert Hayes's concept of world class companies—those that pursue and successfully project a consistent, coherent, and qualitative image to the global marketplace in their products and communications—has the best chance for being achieved if there is an objective evaluation and prescriptive process.

An external audit team introduces the element of managing the process for achieving a coherent corporate image. The team, consisting of recognized experts in product, communications, and environment design, should function on a multiyear basis in order to be thoroughly familiar with the company's goals and operating processes. A sufficient time span is also essential for the consultants to assess progress over a period of time. A prerequisite for the success of a design audit program, in addition to continuity, is the composition of the group of people with whom the audit team interacts. If the contact is limited to those who are directly responsible for design activities, the effort, while certainly better than conducting no sort of audit, will be limited in its potential for what can be achieved. The audit should be seen as a potent activity for obtaining strategic results and, as such, should involve senior managers across the spectrum of strategic functions.

A design audit program does pose an element of threat, especially for design and marketing managers, but such an evaluation process has the possibility to provide a framework for feedback discussions between design managers and marketing managers to assess market results. This end of the product creation process, which ought to be the foundation for future generations of product and communications creation, can be an important element in the mix of design research and product planning activities. Design managers should regard the audit team members as potential allies in helping to secure the resources they may need to improve their design capabilities or for facilitating difficulties in communications with their product and communications creation colleagues in marketing and product development. Marketing managers may need to be persuaded that the audit team's contribution goes well beyond a simple aesthetic critique to providing professional insights into why a product or communications program fell short in achieving what was intended and, even more important, what actions can be taken together with designers to produce results. Skilled consultants will also be able to reinforce a company's commitment to the positive elements of the body of work they evaluate.

For all these reasons, those who participate with the audit team must have some input into their selection. The primary resource for selecting an audit team should be someone who has a good understanding of the company and its problems and goals as well as, quite obviously, current knowledge of a broad range of design consultants and their work. The audit team should be approved and fully supported by the company CEO.

A design audit program, clearly, goes well beyond the normal practice of hiring in a design consultancy to create a "corporate image," which usually means designing a logo program. A design audit program establishes a corporate commitment to managing its resources in order to succeed in becoming a world class, design-coherent company.

SUMMING UP: DESIGN MANAGEMENT COMMON GROUND FOR ALL COMPANIES

The most important thing for any company to recognize, no matter what business you are in, with whom you do your business, or what your size is, is that your company projects an image about what it does. That image—the sum of the company's products and/or services, communications, and the environment in which it operates—will *be* projected whether it is managed or just simply happens. Managing how your company is perceived, which is what a corporate identity program is all about, is, of course, much preferred to letting the chips fall where they may, because you are at least exerting some conscious control over the way your company will be judged. Design management is the activity that marshalls and nurtures the company support and resources for developing and executing a coordinated corporate identity program. The tasks of managing a company's design resources will be much the same for any company. These tasks involve giving leadership by:

- Communicating the strategic importance of design as the framework for a corporate identity program

- Establishing and maintaining the necessary networking relationships to ensure that design is integrated into the stream of research to market activities

Operational aspects of design management are also common to all companies. In general they can be summarized as:

- Deciding how the elements of a corporate identity program (product, communication, and environment design) will be structured. Globalism will affect nearly all companies, as will the increasing trend toward partnerships and joint ventures. These developments are complicating management tasks; this is especially true for design management. A coherent corporate identity program will be increasingly critical as complexity escalates.

- Deciding who will do the design work. There are no rules here, but whether consultants, in-house staff, or a combination of these are the choice, both the choice and the management of the design work require experienced-based design direction.

The individual company will carry out these tasks-in-common in its own way. But clearly, these key activities will be executed to the strategic benefit of the company if they are recognized as the tasks of design management.

CHAPTER NINE

The Fertile Ground Factor

CREATING A CORPORATE CULTURE FOR DESIGN TO FLOURISH

Several years before leaving Herman Miller I sensed some concern among the design consultants associated with the company at the time about whether Herman Miller's commitment to design would be submerged in its rising tide of success in office systems. I thought it was important to discuss these concerns with our consultant and staff designers as well as ideas about how to deal with design and the enormous changes going on at Herman Miller. We agreed to meet retreat-style during and after the Aspen Design Conference. Because our discussions centered on the issue of the company's cultural heritage of design and how to keep that culture alive, we began to refer to our discussions as "fertile ground" meetings.

The fertile ground reference became the shorthand label for what the group, which included Bruce Burdick, Don Chadwick, Jack Tanis, Bill Stumpf, Ralph Caplan, and John Massey, felt needed to be consciously attended to so that Herman Miller would not lose what made it the leader in the furniture industry: its longstanding emphasis on taking risks with innovative designs. Like the patient farmer who plants the seeds, provides water and endless cultivation, and takes actions to counter weeds, pests, disease, and bad weather, a company must also cultivate, nurture, and protect what it does in order to reap a good harvest. But most important, the designers said, before anything of quality can take root and flourish, the ground must be well prepared. You cannot just throw a seed into the ground and hope for the best.

Thus, even in a company celebrated and admired as an example of design excellence, it was understood that because fertile ground existed for design to flourish it would not necessarily always remain so. A sustained effort to keep the ground fertile needed to be consciously made. The passing of the De Pree family from positions of authority and the increase in the number and scope of decision-making managers, many of them new to the company, suggested that the company culture could change.

The fertile ground factor is fundamental to the success of design in any company. Because design is an enabler of research, engineering, production, and marketing, the fertile ground must exist companywide. Design gives tangible form to technology innovations and to product and marketing plans. This means establishing and continuously nurturing a cultural awareness of design and its crucial role as enabler. The fertile ground factor underscores the importance of implanting and cultivating the concept of design excellence as a core value of the company with the care and continuous toil of the patient farmer.

It was noted early in this book that the frequently declared conventional wisdom is that design flourishes most often in companies with a CEO dedicated to lifting its enabling role above the mundane. It was also noted that too often when the visionary CEO passes from the scene, the handoff is fumbled because the receiver does not have the same vision of design. The issue pondered by our fertile ground group at Herman Miller was, how do you spread the commitment through a company to ensure its staying power?

WHAT MAKES THE GROUND FERTILE?

Apart from the occasional and accidental good luck of having a CEO who has an abiding sensitivity to design excellence and the ability to perceive the business sense of the design-as-enabler concept, the fertile ground factor is a responsibility that should be institutionalized as a management function, which is what this book has been all about. The executive manager for design has the responsibility for establishing and nurturing the corporate fertile ground for design. It is an elusive, unquantifiable, and utterly essential task. Its importance is paramount, because it is a prerequisite for instituting a successful corporate identity program.

Fortunately, much is being said without embarrassment these days about the importance of corporate culture as a starting point (fertile ground) for effecting changes in the way company employees think and act. The buzz phrase of the decade is "soft values," describing everything from what is motivating consumers in their purchasing behavior and lifestyles to the inner soul of the corporate body. If it is now acceptable for management teams to spend days together in the wilderness enduring mountain-climbing challenges or white-water-rafting experiences to build team trust, it is probably okay, now that psyches among workmates are being bared, to bring design out of the workplace closet. The complaint that designers have to stop defending design in "designspeak" and speak the language of businesspeople is only half on the mark. Designers, of course, should thoroughly comprehend corporate goals and strategies and place their work contribution within those contexts.

The objective aspects of design should be identified, evaluated, and vigorously communicated. But the soft values of design should neither be given lower priority nor apologized for. An attitude of receptivity to both the objective, hard criteria and the soft values of design is an element of the corporate culture. Like building trust among a work team or fighting fear of risk taking, receptivity to and respect for the soft values of design have to be consciously cultivated.

Building a corporate culture for design is rather obviously a long-term task. And, like the farmer, the design manager has to be constantly vigilant against weeds and pests to protect what has already been established. I see this aspect of design management as a two-tier effort. The first tier is the groundwork that prepares the way for the second tier of receptivity to the soft values of design.

Though Philips had a corporate commitment to design in 1980, as the chapters describing the changes that needed to be made pointed out, a considerable gap existed between the stated commitment and how the design process actually functioned. The significant quality improvement I considered critical was largely necessary because of the prevailing attitudes toward design. The important decisions were made by either the commercial or technical managers, which indicated an underappreciation of the design function and its value to the product creation process.

The harmonization program was, and continues to be, as important as an education medium about the design process as it is for the results it produces. The design workshop concept added an invaluable technique for reinforcing teamwork for product creation. Technical and commercial managers participate at the beginning and end of workshops. The information and briefing sessions are now discussions rather than "handed down" briefings. The videophone project illustrated how the workshop setting was an opportunity for designers to channel the thinking of the engineers and marketing people to consider issues they had not adequately resolved. The sponsorship by CID of the Design to Market workshop was a proactive strategy to position design as an essential player in the product creation process. The successful implementation of the training program for teams, which included designers, to develop a work procedure was clearly identified with CID as the initiator and champion of team building for a better product creation process.

The successful launch of the Philips Collection at the end of 1991 was also an acknowledged design-driven program. Press openings in countries throughout Europe, staged in such prestigious museums as the Vitra Museum in Germany and the Beaubourg in Paris and presented with design-oriented flair at events in Malmo, Milan, Brussels, Zurich, and Tokyo demonstrated that the fertile ground, enriched with a vigorous design process and qualitatively improved products, had moved design awareness to a new level of more holistic thinking. A receptivity to a corporate identity approach was beginning to take root.

COMMUNICATE! COMMUNICATE! COMMUNICATE!

Because CID has always been a far-flung organization, the old newsletter stand-by was one effort to keep the communications lines open. In 1980 the newsletter was the typical dreary rag with dull writing and no visual interest. If CID needed to improve the corporate mentality toward design, everything CID did itself had to express a concern for quality and set an example for ourselves and others in the company. The newsletter, renamed *INFORM,* was completely revamped in its design and content. The focus was on design issues and what CID was doing regarding these matters. At the outset it seemed logical that this information was useful not just within CID but that the newsletter could serve as a valuable design education medium to managers throughout CID. When requests began to come in from far corners of the company to be put on the mailing list, we notched up one small victory for design awareness. The mailing list now numbers 1700.

Siemens publishes a magazine, *Design News.* Its purpose, according to Siemens Chief Designer Herbert Schultes, is to "sensitize awareness of the dangers associated with lacking design compatibility and at the same time provide the information necessary for correct procedure." In addition to using the magazine as a tactic for ensuring that the synergy essential for maintaining a corporate identity is burned into the consciousness of all Siemens managers, he aims to show everyone connected to product design "about the design know-how and creative potential available within the firm."[1] Schultes vividly expresses concern about the effect of decentralization on eroding corporate identity, and he is producing an impressive publication to prop up the design awareness level.

Fluency in making the case for design is frequently mentioned in recent articles about design management as a requisite qualification for design managers. Although such fluency is obviously essential, supplementing one's voice with that of others from outside the company helps a great deal. An effective supplement is to operate a personalized clipping service, sending articles about design with attached notes to targeted product managers or even the president to help to reinforce a point you want to make. For that matter, the article may not be specifically about design but about a demographic or marketing trend or some subject that has a bearing on a point you'd like to make. It boosts your case if someone like Christopher Lorenz in the *Financial Times* or Professor Robert Hayes in the *Harvard Review* provides additional ammunition.

Less direct ways of communicating the design message are limited only by the design manager's imagination and resources. One of the more obvious and time-honored is the design competition. The reasons for taking competitions seriously are not confined to the external publicity awards they may generate. Competition successes offer one more way to communicate to your company peers that someone outside the company values a quality design achievement. Approbation by those outside the "family" usually counts for more than from the inside in the eyes of the family itself. Communicating about competition awards internally is possibly the most important benefit of a competition award, especially if the product creation process was problematic.

The Philips president, Jan Timmer, found a way to communicate a message that was as potent as it was wordless. A program for a television whose design he was devoted to went off the track despite his strong support for the design, my own efforts, and those of the senior managers for television. On a shelf behind Timmer's desk, a large photo of the model is displayed of the stillborn television. Those who were involved with the project, both the champions and the spoilers, see the message with a thousand meanings every time they visit his office. This potent form of communication surely played a part in the eventual revival of the project.

REACHING THE HIGH GROUND: DEDICATION TO A CORPORATE IDENTITY PROGRAM

The Herman Miller holistic approach to design in its corporate identity program, described in the case study section, is a classic example of how sufficient design awareness throughout the company could permit the establishment years ago of a total corporate identity. The ideal situation, the goal to shoot for, is to maintain a quality equilibrium in the component elements of the corporate identity. For very many years Herman Miller was able to do that.

At Philips the ground has been sufficiently prepared in the product design activity and in the design awareness it has generated for more attention to be directed to establishing a true corporate identity program. The Evoluon case study described in Chapter 7 is a significant milestone for Philips, because the Evoluon project was an exercise in the process of lifting the quality level of the corporate identity of Philips. Those who participated in the process at both the decision-making and project work level have undergone a fundamental change in attitude about how the company should see itself and project itself to others in the company as well as its other various constituencies. The corporate culture for design has moved to a broader, more comprehensive level. The Evoluon will stand as a model for everyone at Philips for the quality execution of a corporate identity project. The company's challenge will be to maintain that quality standard at the Evoluon and to transfer its lessons to other corporate design and communications activities.

WHO SHOULD TILL THE FERTILE GROUND?

I return to this subject in conclusion because it is so very important to the successful implanting and execution of the design process in corporations and because it is in danger of being misdirected as the focus on design becomes more intense. The source of misdirection could come from the education institutions that are struggling to produce some sort of design management education.

The concept should be clear at this point that the combination of a CEO who is committed not just to product design but to all the elements of a managed corporate identity program in partnership with a qualified design director functioning in the top echelon of the company's organizational structure is the fundamental requirement for projecting a successful company image and achieving corporate strategic goals. The key phrase in this criterion is *qualified design manager.* The earlier passages describing the tasks of design management and the case studies demonstrating what is involved with managing design should make clear the distinction between managing design and general business management. Yet there is an idea that managing design is something that can be taught to anyone who attends business school. Worse, the idea is taking root, especially in U.K. educational institutions, that if business students follow a program module of design management courses, a growing army of business managers will be capable of making design decisions and are thus qualified to manage design for the companies in which they work.

A group of polytechnics and universities in the United Kingdom has been working with dedication to analyze the needs of industry for design and subsequently to develop design management education programs at both the postgraduate and undergraduate level of business education. The design management modules, which are based on the joint efforts of the Council for National Academic Awards (CNAA) and the United States' Fullbright Commission, are now being taught to some 3000 business school graduates each year. The coursework is intended to have a diffuse influence on improving the relationship between design practice and business management. The ultimate goal is to integrate design management into business curricula so that the long-term effect will raise the level of awareness of the importance of design thereby improving design performance throughout U.K. industry.

Some of the leading proponents of the design curricula for business students are admirers of an interesting and provocative research project conducted by Angela Dumas, now director of the London Business School design management program, and Alan Brickwood, head of design at Teeside Polytechnic in the United Kingdom. A paper written by Angela Dumas and Peter Gorb based on this research describes the findings of the Dumas/Brickwood work.[2] Basically what Dumas found out was that "design activity pervades organizations and that it is dispersed, interactive and frequently undertaken by people who would not recognize that their job involves design." Dumas coined this inadvertent activity "silent design." She raises questions she says need further study regarding the relationship between *silent design* (which she also refers to as covert design, suggesting that the activity is not quite so innocently unconscious as it is declared to be by its practitioners) and *overt design management.* she also wonders if there can be an optimum balance between the two.

The well-intentioned U.K. educators have made some assumption leaps, perhaps in part influenced by the findings of Dumas and Brickwood. Louis van Praag, one of the activists for establishing design education for business students, declared in a discussion reported by the Royal Society for the Arts that he was against creating a new discipline called "design management." Rather, the goal of design management education, he thinks, should be to acquaint managers of companies with the concept of design management in the hope that they will see it to that this activity is properly conducted. While this in itself is a worthwhile goal, my worst nightmare is one in which tens or hundreds of business school graduates will consider themselves qualified to make design decisions because they have taken a few courses in design management.

As a design manager with nearly 40 years of direct experience in industry I believe to the depths of my soul that silent design doesn't work. Nor do covert design decisions made by nondesigners work. I have had interaction with product planners, advertising managers, design engineers, production engineers, facility managers—the list goes on—nearly every day of my working life, who were silent designers. Very often they were making covert design decisions. In the vast majority of these situations these "end run" actions resulted in design decisions that ultimately raised project costs, reduced product quality, or produced support materials and communications that were incompatible with the product. However, when design decisions were orchestrated between design, marketing, and production the desired results were achieved, as many of the Philips and Herman Miller case studies demonstrate. The Harvard/Design Management Institute TRIAD project gives further evidence of the value of a successful design management role in orchestrating the design creation process.

What is called for is a double-barreled approach to the silent design syndrome cited by Dumas and Brickwood and the call from diverse and widespread sources for the upgrading of the design role in business and industry. A component on design should absolutely be a required part of every business student's education. But the emphasis should be on raising students' awareness of the importance of design and on communicating an understanding of the design process and its integral role in product creation and in creating corporate identity. The goal should be to create receptivity to *interaction* with design and for students to understand enough about the process to respect the point at which *design decisions should be made by designers.*

The second part of the education approach is to provide design management education to designers. These programs should be integrated into business schools, with the emphasis on general management coursework, so that designers can manage the interaction process, manage resources, and polish up their communication techniques for their predictable task of persuasion. The ideal candidate for such a design management program is a designer with at least four or five years of credible design work experience. Another source for candidates is the career-change designer. I have observed a number of designers who were either burned out from their youthful creativity or perhaps were only moderately successful designers but who had the potential to be effective design managers. The fortyish designer on staff who fits this description is someone companies should look at for sponsorship to a design management program.

I believe that design matters should be in the hands of designers. Although many nondesigners can be sensitive to and supportive of design matters and absolutely essential to the success of design in companies, relatively few should be making design decisions. Increasing the number of nondesigner enablers of design is the desirable goal rather than making designers out of every business student.

I have already described the layers of education and, more important, experience which feed the decisions design managers must make. My years of interaction with work associates at all levels and from every area of company activity have brought me to a conclusion about the issue of nondesigners and their capabilities to make design decisions: I think there are three levels of visual acuity. The first level includes the majority of people. These people visit the Parthenon or see a Picasso painting in a museum. They nod and say, yes, I can understand something about why this has been judged "good." At the second level of visual acuity there are far fewer people. These people can look at a critically acclaimed painting by, say, David Salle, or a chair design by Ettore Sottsass and say, "I'm sorry, I don't like it. I don't agree with the critical judgment." But these people will be able to know why they have reached an independent decision because they have spent some time studying art or design history and kept abreast of current developments. At the third level, the numbers thin out dramatically. This is the level at which someone is confronted with an object, a model, or a layout about which no critical judgment has been made. This is the level at which visual acuity with its mix of right-brain dominance, informed reference points, and layers of experience operates at its keenest. This is what the designer spends his or her lifetime developing.

Certainly in the practical course of business, few project decisions are based purely on design decisions. But the designer or design manager should be able to enter the decision negotiation process from the integrity of a respected design position. The much vaunted interaction doesn't mean anything if the design component is based on decisions over which designers have no control.

Finally, the theme throughout this book is about something that most certainly has no place in silent design. It is about design leadership. The pivot point for design as an enabler for a company's technology developments, production processes, marketing plans, and communications is a vision of what design excellence should be and how that vision is communicated throughout the organization. This pivot turns on how effectively and skillfully design is integrated into the design-to-market stream of activities.

Design leadership means raising the noise level in the company about design, countering the naïvete of unconscious, silent design. It confronts usurping the designer's rightful role in covert design decision making.

Above all, design leadership is about communicating an evangelistic passion for excellence in the quality of all the things that forge the company's image: the products the company creates; the visual symbols with which it identifies itself; the advertising, packaging, exhibitions, public relations with which the company promotes itself; how the company communicates to its employees and shareholders; the attention the company pays to the quality of its workplace. These are the crown jewels of a company. Design leadership is about never letting the company forget about the value of those jewels.

REFERENCES

1. Herbert H. Schultes, *Design News,* Siemens Design Information, Siemens Aktiengesellschaft, Berlin and Munich, 1991.

2. Peter Gorb and Angela Dumas, "Silent Design," *Design Studies,* vol. 8, no. 3, July 1987, published in cooperation with the Design Research Society.

Index

Note: An *f.* after a page number refers to a figure.

Action Office 2 (AO2), 54–55, 57
   research, user needs, 73–74
Added value, 9, 35–36, 67
Albinson, Don, 64
Amanuma, Aki, 26
Ambasz, Emilio, 58, 171, 173
American Center for Design, 29
Apple, 22, 33, 38
Ashby, Gordon, 64
Atjak, Antonio, 134, 136–137, 142
Audit:
   design, 174–176

Bang & Olufsen, 22
Bauer, Dale, 64
Beaubourg Museum, 154, 180
Beeren, Lou, 125 *f.*
Bel Geddes, Norman, 94–95
Bellini, Mario, 171
Bock & Dekker Group, 135–136
Braun, 22
Brickwood, Alan, 110, 183–184
Burdick, Bruce, 55, 57, 105, 157–161, 178
   Burdick System, 55, 57
Burdick, Susan, 105, 159–161
Buter, Reinhart, 105

Camens, Murray, 129–130
Canon, 169
Caplan, Ralph, 35, 48, 79, 178
CBS, 33
Centralization:
   of design functions, 97–98, 113–114,
     168–170
Chadwick, Don, 55–56, 178
Charles, Barbara, 157

Clark, Kim, 127
Communications:
   about design, 166, 181–182
   design, 9
   design media, 23
Competitive advantage, 36
Computer-Aided Design (CAD), 106–107, 149,
     150–151, 168
Consultant designers:
   at Herman Miller, 55, 57–58, 172
   management of, 14, 170
   at Philips, 105, 108–109, 143–148, 172–174
Consumers:
   empowerment of, 20, 21
   (*See also* User needs)
Container Corporation, 33
Cooper Hewitt Museum, 29
Corporate design resources:
   management of, 37–38, 80, 146–147,
     150–152, 155–156, 173–174
Corporate goals:
   design as a strategic factor of, 34, 162, 165
Corporate identity:
   definition of, 8
   and design policy, 14
   and environment, 34
   at Herman Miller, 49–50, 81–86, 182
   management of, 38
   at Philips, 110, 161–162, 182
   strategic importance of, 170, 176
   tasks of, 161
Corporate strategy, 34, 63, 67, 80, 85, 123, 127,
     133, 138, 151, 162

Decentralization:
   of design, 38–39, 97–98, 113–117, 166–170
Dekker, Wisse, 94, 158

Deming, W. Edwards, 39
De Pree, D. J., 47–50, 52–53
De Pree, Hugh, 48, 52–55, 71, 74, 166
De Pree, Max, 48, 57
Design:
    "Champion," 33, 179–180, 183
    codification of, 8
    as core competency, 97
    and corporate culture, 179–180
    creating change, management of, 8
    limits of, 12, 35–36
    methodology, 8
    organizational structure of, 166–170
    portfolio responsibility, 10, 39–41,
        183–186
    process period of, 22
Design leadership, 168, 185–186
Design management:
    definition of, 13, 38
    education, 183–186
    at Herman Miller, 60–86
    issues, 32–44, 183–184
    mission of, 165
    at Philips, 180
    tasks of, 13–17, 166, 168, 172, 176
Design Management Institute (DMI), 30
Design manager:
    education of, 40, 42–43, 182–186
    experience of, 40, 182–186
    qualifications of, 39–41, 64–65,
        182–186
    role of, 13, 128
    tasks of, 113, 166, 176–177, 179
Design for Market:
    Philips program, 124–127
Design policy, 14, 16, 99
Design process:
    management of, 15, 32, 180
Design resources:
    management of, 14–16, 37–38, 81–86
Design research, 60, 65, 73–74
    in Japan, 24–27
    (See also User needs)
Design-to-market process, 9, 64
Design work:
    scope of, 33–36, 63, 66–67, 71, 80, 135–138,
        151, 165, 177
Dictaphone, 171
Differentiation:
    of products, 20, 148–151
    for youth, 128–133
Diffrient, Niels, 105–106, 174
Digital Equipment Corporation, 171

Doblin, Jay, 135
Donges, Dick, 64
Dumas, Angela, 110, 183–184

Eames, Charles, 12, 32, 50–52, 55, 60, 81, 158,
    166, 172
    Contract Storage (ECS), 60–65
    Educational Seating (EES), 51, 65–68
    Executive Seating, 52
    Soft Pad Seating, 52
    Tandem Seating, 51–52, 69–73
Eames, Ray, 52, 81–82
Education:
    of design managers, 42, 183–186
    of designers, 40
    skill upgrading, 15, 105
Engineering design:
    relationship with industrial design, 10–11
    methodology, 35
Environment design, 9–10, 85
Eppinger, Jimmy, 50
Erco Lighting Company, 171
Ergonomics, 106, 149
Esprit, 22

Fahnstrom, Dale, 144–146
Fehlbaum, Willie, 57
Financial Times:
    conference, "Product Strategies for the '90s,"
        26, 30
Finland:
    University of Industrial Arts Helsinki
        (UIAH), 28
Fitch, Richardson, Smith, 105, 172
Fleetwood, Roy, 171
France:
    support for design, 27–28
Frog Design/Germany, 144–146
Frykholm, Stephen, 84

Generalist, designers as, 16–17, 64–65
Germany:
    support for design, 28
Girard, Alexander, 81–83
Global design organization:
    management of, 38–39, 97–98, 167–170
Global products, 34, 131f., 132, 148–151
Globalism, 19–20, 176
Gorb, Peter, 8–9, 40–41, 110, 125, 126f., 183
Gross margin performance, 9

Haller, Fritz, 57–58
Harmonization:
    of product design, 118–124
        goals of, 119
Hayes, Robert H., 22, 175, 181
Herman Miller:
    communications program, 81–86
    consultants, 55, 57–58, 170
    corporate identity, 49–50, 81–86
    design "champion," 33
    facilities design, 82–83
    holistic design program, 22, 38, 182
    house style program, 83
    human resource management, 85–86
    internal design staff, 55, 80
    portfolio responsibility for design, 85–86
    product planning, 52–53
Heskett, John, 95, 138
Hinde, Grahm, 129–130
Holistic design, 22, 182
Hollein, Hans, 58

IBM, 22, 33, 38
Idea sources, of designers, 15–16
Industrial Design Society of America (IDSA),
    33
Information network, 15–16
In-house design staff, 55, 80, 143–147,
    170–174
Innovation:
    design-led, 36–37, 67–68, 72–73, 124,
        134–147
    incremental refinements, 51
Integration of design:
    element of strategic operations, 165
    into organizational structure, 12–13
    into product creation process, 36, 80,
        124–128, 134, 140, 147, 185
Interaction design, 35, 106, 109
Interdisciplinary team, 15, 106, 109, 124–127,
    140–142
International Council of Societies of Industrial
    Designers (ICSID), 24, 27
Issues, design management, 32–44
    design, status of in corporation, 33–34, 71,
        113, 143
    design-led innovation, 36–37, 72–73, 124,
        134, 147
    design manager:
        education of, 40, 42–43, 183–186
        qualifications, 39–41, 64–65, 183–186
        status of, 33

Issues, design management (*Cont.*):
    design resources, management of, 37–38, 80,
        86, 146–147, 151, 154–155
    global organization, management of, 38–39,
        167–170
    integration in product creation process, 36,
        80, 127–128, 134, 147
    quality, design as a force for, 39, 73, 85, 124,
        155, 167–168
    scope of design work, 35–36, 63, 67, 71, 80,
        85, 138, 151
    strategic factor, 34, 63, 67, 80, 86, 123, 127,
        133–134, 138, 151, 155, 161–162

Japan:
    competition from, 23, 27
    G Mark Award, 23–24
    Japanese Industrial Design Promotion
        Organization (JIDPO), 23–24, 26–27
    Ministry of International Trade and Industry
        (MITI), 23–24
Jeelof, Gerritt, 118, 124, 166
Jones, Quincy, 83
Juran, J. M., 39

Kalff, Louis, 94
Keeley, Larry, 135
King, Perry, 105
Kjaerholm, Paul, 57–58
von Klier, Hans, 171
van der Klugt, Cornelius, 96, 128, 158
Korea:
    support for design, 24
Kotler, Philip, 35–36
Krippendorf, Klaus, 105

Labohm, Fons, 155
Lawrence, Peter, 124, 126*f.*
Lee, Hon Son, 130, 132
van Leeuwen, Leo, 129
Lifestyle research, 14, 24–26
    model for, 65
Line managers:
    interface with design, 13
Lippenkhof, Johnny, 122, 144–145
Loewy, Raymond, 21, 93
London Business School:
    design management program, 41, 183
London Design Center, 28, 30

Lorenz, Christopher, 18, 181
De Lucchi, Michele, 171

Maack, Klaus-Jurgen, 171–172
Market segmentation, 20
Massey, John, 83, 178
Matrix analysis, 134–138
Mauro, Charles, 105
McArthur, John H., 30, 32
McCoy, Katherine, 105
McCoy, Michael, 105, 122, 144–146
Media:
   interest in design, 23
Meikle, Jeffrey, 39
Meyer, Thierry, 162
Miller, Jeffrey, 124, 126f.
Miranda, Santiago, 105
Moggridge, Bill, 105, 172
Morgue, Olivier, 57
van Mourik, Arthur, 158

Nakanishi, Motoo, 25–26
National Endowment for the Arts, 29
Nelson, George, 22, 49–50, 52, 55, 75, 81–83,
   86, 172
Networking, 15–16, 165, 168, 176
Newman, Frank, 148–149
Noyes, Elliot, 22

Ockeloen, Gijs, 138–141, 143
Olivetti, 33, 171
Organizational structure:
   of design, 166–170
      at Herman Miller, 166–167
      at Philips, 97–98, 100–101f., 113–115,
         116–117f., 166–167
Ottens, Lou, 125–127
Owen, Ivor, 11

Panton, Vernor, 57–58
Paulin, Pierre, 58
Peterson, Donald E., 12
Philips:
   corporate identity, 110–113, 161–162, 182
   Corporate Industrial Design (CID):
      accountability, 102–103
      consultants, 105, 108–109, 172–175
      decentralization, 97, 113, 116–117f.,
         168–170

Philips, Corporate Industrial Design (CID)
   (Cont.):
      design policy, 99
      recruitment, 103–105
      restructuring, 97–98, 100–101f.
      workshops, 107–110, 144–149
   goals:
      of design program, 97–98
   harmonization program, 110–111, 113,
      118–124
   holistic design program, 22, 182
   house style, 111–112
Plumb, Bill, 105
Powell, Earl, 15
Process period:
   of design, 22
Product creation process, 11 f., 36, 124–128,
   175, 180
Product management:
   difference from design management,
      64
Product planning, 128, 134–138, 169
Profitability:
   design as a factor for, 9
Propst, Robert, 52–55, 172
   Action Factory, 58
   Action Office, 54–55, 58, 73–80
   Coherent Structures, 58
van der Put, Frans, 98

Quality, 15
   design as a force for, 39, 68, 73, 85, 124, 155,
      167–168, 181
   "designed-in," 62, 68
   and design policy, 99

Recruitment:
   of designers, 103–105, 168
Regionalism, 19
Responsibility:
   distributing, 98–99, 100–101f.
Rheinfrank, John, 105, 172
Robinson, Cameron, 130
Rohde, Gilbert, 49
Ruch, Dick, 76

Saarinen, Eero, 71
Sakashita, Kiyoshi, 26, 169–170, 173
Schultes, Herbert, 181
Schultze-bahr, Werner, 122

Schwartz, Joe, 76, 79
Seki, Yasuko, 25
Sharp, 26, 169–170, 173
Siemens, 181
"Silent" design, 110, 183–185
Singapore:
   support for design, 24, 28
Snoey, Steven, 76
Sony, 22, 26, 33, 38, 169
Sottsass, Ettore, Jr., 171, 185
Spain:
   support for design, 28
Staples, Bob, 64, 67, 68, 158
Status:
   of design in corporations, 33–34, 71, 113,
     143
Sterkenberg, Huug, 119
Strategic planning:
   integration of design, 9
   needs-based, 14
Stubsjoen, Harvey, 69
Stumpf, Bill, 178
Stuttgart Design Center, 28
Styling, 21–22
System design, 34, 118–124

Taiwan:
   support for design, 24
Tanis, Jack, 178
Tasks:
   design management, 13–17, 113
     capital resource management, 38
     corporate identity management, 38
     financial resource management, 38
     human resource management, 37
Thackera, John, 110, 112
Timmer, Jan, 111, 152–153, 160, 162, 166,
   182
TRIAD project, 15, 30, 138
"Turfism," 11–12, 36

United Kingdom:
   support for design, 28–29
United States:
   support for design, 29
User interface, 35, 138–141
User needs:
   designer concern for, 136–138
   identification of, 14, 21
     lifestyle research, 14
   research, 65
   (*See also* Design research)

Values, "hard," 8–9
Values, "soft," 8–9, 21, 24–25, 179–180
Veeneklaas, Just, 111
Veersma, Rein, 94
Visual literacy, 41
Vitra Design Museum, 155, 180
Vranken, Bob, 129

Walters, Glenn, 76
Wasserman, Arnold, 26–27
Weisz, Sandor, 171
Workshops:
   consultants, use of, 105, 109, 144–148
   and design research, 108
   skill upgrading, 105–110
   and technology application, 108–109
   work methodology, 107–110, 144–148, 149,
     169
World class company:
   definition of, 22
Woudhuysen, James, 105

Yamaha, 169
Yran, Knut, 94–95, 104

About the Authors

DR. ROBERT BLAICH, now a design management consultant, was senior managing director of Corporate Industrial Design at Philips Electronics of the Netherlands, one of the world's leading producers of electronic products. Previously, he was vice president of design and development at Herman Miller, Inc., an international leader in the design and manufacture of furniture systems.

A Fellow of the Industrial Designer's Society of America and Royal Society of the Arts, Mr. Blaich is past president of the International Council of Societies of Industrial Design. He was awarded an honorary degree in fine arts by Syracuse University and named an officer in the Order of Oranje Nassau, the equivalent of a knighthood, by Queen Beatrix of the Netherlands. Dr. Blaich is currently professor of design management at leading universities in Europe and the United States and consultant to European, Asian, and American corporations and governments.

JANET BLAICH has been a newspaper editorial writer, magazine publisher and editor, and corporate speech writer. She has written about design for professional journals and collaborates with her husband, Robert, in developing speeches about design management.